Table of Contents

Introduction to the Common Core State Standards
Grade 5

Why Are Common Core State Standards Important for My Child?
The Common Core State Standards are a set of guidelines that outline what children are expected to learn at school. Most U.S. states have voluntarily adopted the standards. Teachers, principals, and administrators in these states use the standards as a blueprint for classroom lessons, district curriculum, and statewide tests. The standards were developed by a state-led collaboration between the Council of Chief State School Officers (CCSSO) and the National Governors Association (NGA).

The Common Core Standards set high expectations for your child's learning. They are up-to-date with 21st century technology and draw on the best practices of excellent schools around the world. They focus on important skills in reading, language arts, and math. Common Core State Standards aim to ensure that your child will be college and career ready by the end of high school and able to compete in our global world.

SPECTRUM®
Common Core
Language Arts and Math

Grade
5

Published by Spectrum®
An imprint of Carson-Dellosa Publishing LLC
Greensboro, North Carolina

Spectrum®
An imprint of Carson-Dellosa Publishing LLC
P.O. Box 35665
Greensboro, NC 27425 USA

Printed in the USA • All rights reserved.   ISBN 978-1-4838-0453-8
02-146141151

What Are the Common Core State Standards for My Fifth Grade Student?

Common Core State Standards for your fifth grader are designed to build a solid foundation for reading, literacy, and mathematical understanding. On practice pages in this book, you will find references to specific Common Core Standards that teachers will expect your child to know by the end of the year. Completing activities on these pages will help your child master essential skills for success in fifth grade.

A Sample of Common Core Language Arts Skills for Grade 5

- Quote accurately from a text.
- Compare and contrast stories in the same genre, such as mysteries or adventure stories.
- Use information from multiple sources to answer questions or write about a topic.
- Write to give an opinion, provide information, or tell a story.
- Use commas to separate items in a series.
- Explain the meanings of common proverbs and adages.

A Sample of Common Core Math Skills for Grade 5

- Generate numerical patterns, use them to find number pairs, and plot the pairs on a grid.
- Move the decimal point in numbers when multiplying by 10, 100, or 1000.
- Multiply and divide multi-digit numbers.
- Solve word problems with fractions.
- Convert measurements (example: from inches to feet).
- Find the volume of rectangular prisms (box shapes).

© Copyright 2010. National Governors Association Center for Best Practices and Council of Chief State School Officers. All rights reserved.

How to Use This Book

In this book, you will find a complete **Common Core State Standards Overview** for fifth grade English Language Arts (pages 6–9) and Math (pages 64–67). Read these pages to learn more about the Common Core Standards and what you can expect your child to learn at school this year.

Then, choose **Practice Pages** that best address your child's needs for building skills that meet specific standards. Help your child complete practice pages and check the answers.

At the bottom of each practice page, you will find a **Helping at Home** tip that provides fun and creative ideas for additional practice with the skill at home.

Common Core State Standards for English Language Arts*

The following parent-friendly explanations of fifth grade Common Core English language arts standards are provided to help you understand what your child will learn in school this year. Practice pages listed will help your child master each skill.

Complete Common Core State Standards may be found here: www.corestandards.org.

RL/RI.5 Reading Standards for Literature and Informational Text

Key Ideas and Details
(Standards: RL.5.1, RL.5.2, RL.5.3, RI.5.1, RI.5.2, RI.5.3)

Your child will quote from a text to answer questions and to explain what the text says directly as well as what can be inferred (or guessed) based on the text.
- **Practice pages: 10, 11, 14, 15, 18, 19, 23–33**

Your child will determine the theme or main idea of a story or nonfiction article. He or she will explain how details from the text support the theme or main idea. Your child will practice summarizing what he or she reads. • **Practice pages: 14–17, 20, 21, 23, 32–35**

Your child will compare and contrast two or more characters, settings, or events from a story.
- **Practice pages: 10–13, 18–21**

When reading nonfiction texts about history, science, and technology, your child will use evidence from the text to explain relationships between people, events, and ideas. For example, he or she might compare and contrast the discoveries of two different inventors.
- **Practice pages: 26, 27, 30, 31**

Craft and Structure
(Standards: RL.5.4, RL.5.5, RL.5.6, RI.5.4, RI.5.5, RI.5.6)

Your child will study and define words and phrases found in texts. For fiction texts, words will include metaphors, similes, and other examples of figurative language. In nonfiction texts, they will include words related to social studies and other content areas.
- **Practice pages: 10, 11, 14–17, 22, 26, 27, 34, 35**

Your child will explain how scenes in a play, stanzas in a poem, or chapters in a novel fit together to tell a story. • **Practice pages: 14, 15**

© Carson-Dellosa • CD-704505

Your child will read two or more nonfiction texts and compare and contrast how information is organized in each. For example, one text might be organized chronologically (by time order). Another might be organized by cause and effect. • **Practice pages: 30, 31**

Your child will study point of view and determine who is telling a story or providing information. He or she will think about how point of view influences the way events are described. Your child will read multiple accounts of the same event and find similarities and differences based on point of view. • **Practice pages: 10–13, 36, 37**

Integration of Knowledge and Skills
(Standards: RL.5.7, RL.5.9, RI.5.7, RI.5.8, RI.5.9)

Your child will think about how illustrations or other visuals contribute to the meaning, tone, or beauty of a text. • **Practice pages: 16, 17**

Your child will use information from multiple sources to answer a question or solve a problem. • **Practice pages: 26–29**

Your child will explain how an author uses reasons and evidence to back up his or her points. • **Practice pages: 23–25**

Your child will compare and contrast different stories in the same genre. For example, he or she will compare two mystery stories or two adventure stories. • **Practice pages: 20, 21**

Your child will combine information from several texts in order to speak or write knowledgeably about a topic. • **Practice pages: 32, 33, 36, 37**

W.5 Writing Standards

Text Types and Purposes
(Standards: W.5.1, W.5.2, W.5.3)

Your child will state an opinion in writing, giving reasons and information to support the opinion. • **Practice pages: 38, 39**

Your child will write to provide facts and information about a topic. • **Practice pages: 32, 33, 41–43**

Your child will write stories with descriptive details and clear sequences of events. • **Practice pages: 44–47**

Common Core State Standards for English Language Arts*

Production and Distribution of Writing
(Standards: W.5.5, W.5.6)

Your child will revise and edit writing to make sure it is correct, to make it more interesting, and to answer questions from readers. • **Practice page: 40**

Your child will use technology, including the Internet, to produce and publish writing. He or she will learn keyboarding skills. • **Practice page: 40**

Research to Build and Present Knowledge
(Standards: W.5.7, W.5.8, W.5.9)

Your child will gather ideas for writing by using a variety of sources to conduct research. Your child will take research notes and create a list of sources. • **Practice page: 42**

Your child will write about what he or she is reading. For example, your child will write to compare and contrast two characters from a story or write to explain ideas from a nonfiction article. • **Practice page: 48**

L.5 Language Standards

Conventions of Standard English
(Standards: L.5.1a, L.5.1b, L.5.1c, L.5.1d, L.5.1e, L.5.2a,
L.5.2b, L.5.2c, L.5.2d, L.5.2e)

Your child will learn to use conjunctions (example: and), prepositions (example: from) and interjections (example: Wow!) correctly in sentences. • **Practice pages: 49–51**

Your child will use perfect verb tenses (examples: I had played, I have played, I will have played) to describe an action that has been—or will be—completed. • **Practice page: 52**

Your child will use verb tenses correctly to tell when actions occur. He or she will practice keeping all verbs in the same tense when writing. • **Practice page: 53**

Your child will use correlative conjunctions (examples: either/or, neither/nor) correctly in sentences. • **Practice page: 54**

Your child will use commas to separate items in a series (example: red, white, and blue). • **Practice page: 55**

Your child will use commas after an introductory element (example: This afternoon, we will finally see the show), to set off the words yes or no (example: Yes, I will go), and to indicate direct address (Is that you, Mom?). • **Practice pages: 50, 56**

Your child will use quotation marks, underlining, or italics for the titles of poems, songs, books, and other works. • **Practice page: 57**

Your child will check spelling carefully, using a dictionary when needed to look up the spellings of words. • **Practice page: 58**

Knowledge of Language
(Standards: L.5.3a, L.5.3b)

Your child will revise sentences, making them longer or shorter or changing words to make sure they have the desired meaning, tone, and style. • **Practice page: 59**

Your child will examine the way that characters speak in stories and plays. He or she will notice regional dialects and other language differences. • **Practice pages: 14, 15, 60**

Vocabulary Acquisition and Use
(Standards: L.5.4a, L.5.4c, L.5.5a, L.5.5b, L.5.5c)

Your child will search the surrounding text for context clues to the meaning of an unknown word. • **Practice pages: 10, 11, 26, 27, 34, 35**

Your child will use dictionaries and other resources to find the pronunciations and definitions of words. • **Practice page: 61**

Your child will study similes (example: as pretty as a picture), metaphors (example: the wind was a bully), and other examples of figurative language. • **Practice pages: 16, 17, 22**

Your child will study common idioms (example: It's raining cats and dogs), adages, and proverbs (example: Nothing ventured, nothing gained). • **Practice page: 62**

Your child will use relationships between words to better understand the meaning of each word. For example, he or she will use the synonym angry *to better understand the meaning of* outraged. • **Practice page: 63**

Comparing Characters

Read the story.

River Climbing

Standing knee-deep in the cold rapids, I watched the river carry leaves, sticks, and a few bird feathers. It felt as if the river wanted to carry me, too.

"Let go of the tree branch, Jess," Jim said.

Jim was squatting on a big rock in the middle of the river. Jim was big and strong; he seemed afraid of nothing. He was always trying to convince me that I was as brave as he was. When I was in third grade, Jim told me that I could jump off the roof of our shed and land on my feet, but he was wrong. I ended up with my leg in a cast. Maybe Jim was wrong about river climbing too—that is what Jim called this quest we were on.

Jim was yelling to me, cheering for me like he did when I teetered on top of that old roof. I fought my way upstream against the water to make it to him. But, the water seemed colder than usual, and the river acted hungry, as if it wanted to eat me. I stubbed my toe, but I could not feel it because I was numb from the knees down. I was getting tired, and I guess that Jim could tell because he told me to hurry.

"Come on, Jess, don't be such a slowpoke," he teased.

I glared at Jim, clenched my teeth, and pushed my body through the water toward him. As I stepped, I slipped on a slimy rock and twisted my ankle. Pain shot up my leg as I lost my balance and tumbled into the freezing current. I stopped fighting and let the river take me away.

"Where are you going?" Jim yelled. "Come on; get up and try again!"

I ignored him and floated to the side of the river, where I grabbed another tree branch. I pulled my body out of the water and lay on the riverbank, inviting the sun to warm me. Then, I found an easier way upstream. I limped barefoot through the shallow water across some stones and sticks to where Jim lay on the rocks. My ankle still hurt from twisting it, but I did not show that I was hurting. My wet clothes stuck to my body.

(to be continued . . .)

Comparing Characters

After reading "River Climbing" (page 10), answer the questions.

1. Who is telling the story?_____

2. What evidence from the story supports your answer to question 1?

_____

_____

3. Complete the Venn diagram to compare and contrast Jess and Jim.

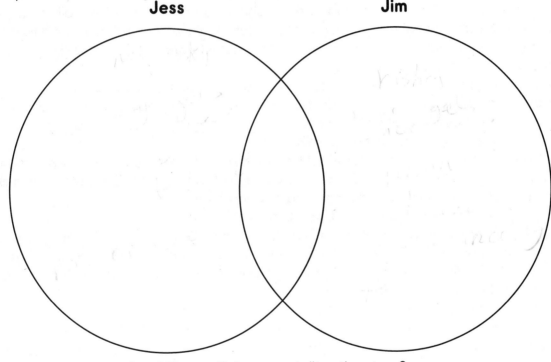

Jess   **Jim**

4. How would the story be different if Jim were telling the story?

_____

_____

5. What are *rapids*? Use clues from the story to help you understand the meaning.

_____

Helping at Home

Ask your child to recount a favorite scene from a book or movie. From whose perspective is the story told? Ask your child to choose another character from the story. How would the scene be different from that character's point of view?

Point of View

Read the story.

River Climbing
(continued from page 10)

I imagined standing under the sun-warmed waterfall that wound through a craggy rock wall nearby. It was the prize for conquering the river climb.

I did not tell Jim that my ankle hurt from my earlier fall; I thought that he would just tell me to stop being a baby. Instead, I made it to the riverbank and climbed onto the dry rocks. While Jim scrambled ahead, I climbed steadily. Finally, I reached the top, where Jim was yodeling from under the falls.

"You made it!" Jim yelled over the sound of the rushing water. I sat near the falls on a slimy rock to catch my breath. I watched Jim play in the waterfall. He wove back and forth like a snake through the rocks on the wall beside the waterfall. He and the water were dancing, turning, and falling. I wished that I were as brave as he was.

Suddenly, Jim began to slip on the slick rocks. He reached out, trying to balance himself, but there was nothing for him to hold onto. I watched Jim's legs buckle under him, and before I knew it, the rush of water pushed him down the mountain of bulging rocks. I saw the blur of his body under the surging water as he fell down the falls.

Without thinking, I rushed to Jim and asked him if he was all right. He had a cut on his forehead, and his leg was bent at an odd angle. I watched him try to move and then yelp like a hurt puppy. He opened his eyes, closed them, and opened them again.

"Jess, help me," he managed to say, looking at me with frightened eyes.

I helped him get to a dry spot on the grass and tried to make him as comfortable as possible. He looked small, not like the Jim I knew. I did not want to leave him, but I knew that I needed to get help. When I finally made it home, I ran inside and told my parents about Jim. Dad and I headed to where Jim lay by the waterfall.

The next day, I woke up early. As I got out of bed, I felt a sharp pain in my ankle. I got dressed quickly, went to Jim's room, and limped fearfully to the side of his bed. Sitting on the edge of his bed, I touched the cast on Jim's broken leg. Jim groaned as he moved his body a little. Then, he opened his eyes.

"Hey, Jess," he said. "Thanks for your help yesterday. You are one brave girl."

© Carson-Dellosa • CD-704505

Point of View

After reading "River Climbing" (pages 10 and 12), answer the questions.

1. How did the roles reverse for Jim and Jess in this part of the story?

_____

_____

2. Were you surprised that Jess is a girl? Explain.

_____

_____

3. Would it have changed what you thought about Jess if you knew she was a girl from the beginning of the story? Explain.

_____

_____

4. How would the story have been different if Jim was telling it?

_____

_____

5. How would the story have been different if a third-person narrator was telling it?

_____

_____

Ask your child to explain how the author shows that Jim is brave. How does the author show that Jess is brave? In the end, which character is braver? Challenge your child to think of other familiar characters that show bravery.

Reading Poetry

Read the poem.

Eldorado
by Edgar Allan Poe

Gaily bedight,
A gallant knight,
In sunshine and in shadow,
Had journeyed long,
Singing a song,
In search of Eldorado.

But he grew old—
This knight so bold—
And o'er his heart a shadow
Fell as he found
No spot of ground
That looked like Eldorado.

And, as his strength
Failed him at length,
He met a pilgrim shadow—
"Shadow," said he,
"Where can it be—
This land of Eldorado?"

"Over the Mountains
Of the Moon,
Down the Valley of the Shadow,
Ride, boldly ride,"
The shade replied,—
"If you seek for Eldorado!"

Reading Poetry

After reading the poem "Eldorado" (page 14), answer the questions.

1. The phrase "gaily bedight, a gallant knight" reflects the language of the time the poem was written. Circle the phrase that best restates the phrase in the language of a fifth grader today. Use a dictionary if needed.

   A. a happy, sleepy, nobleman

   B. a bright, sleepy soldier

   C. brightly dressed, a brave soldier

   D. happily dressed, a nobleman

2. Explain how the author uses repetition in each stanza.

   _____

   _____

3. Why does the author divide the poem into stanzas?

   _____

   _____

4. What happens to the knight in the poem? Quote a phrase to support your answer.

   _____

   _____

5. El Dorado is a legendary golden city that is filled with treasure and precious jewels. Many explorers have searched for the city, but it has never been found. Knowing this, what do you think Poe's message is in "Eldorado"?

   _____

   _____

Helping at Home

Challenge your child to write another stanza for the poem that describes Eldorado. Read and admire your child's writing. Ask him or her to explain how the new stanza is similar to and different from the first four. Does the new stanza fit well? Why?

Finding Imagery

Read the story.

The Hero of Harlem
by Sara Cone Bryant (adapted)

Long ago, a boy named Hans lived in a small town in Holland called Harlem. One day, Hans took his little brother out to play to the edge of the town near the dike. As the boys were playing, the little brother commented, "Look, Hans, the dike has a hole."

Hans looked at the hole in the dike and saw a drop of water bubbling slowly through the hole. He knew that all the water needed was a little hole, and soon, it would burst through the dike, flooding the whole town. Almost without thinking, Hans stuck his finger into the hole and told his little brother to run to town and warn the townspeople that there was a hole in the dike.

For a long time, Hans knelt with his finger in the hole in the dike. His hand began to feel numb, and the cold began to creep up his arm. It seemed as if hours had gone by since his brother left. He stared down the road, straining to see someone, but there was no one.

As his ear touched the dike, he thought he heard the voice of the ocean murmuring, "I am the great sea. No one can stand against me. You are only a little boy. Do you think that you can keep me out?"

Hans instinctively started to pull his finger from the dike to run before the sea broke through, and it was too late to escape. He thought of the sea bursting through the dike and imagined a great flood spreading far over the land, leaving ruin in its wake. As he thought of this, he gritted his teeth and shoved his finger into the dike tighter than before.

At that moment, he heard a shout. In the distance, he saw the townspeople dashing down the road carrying pickaxes and shovels. "Hold on! We're coming!" they shouted.

It seemed like only a moment before the crowd was there. When they saw Hans with his finger wedged tightly into the hole in the dike, they gave a robust cheer. When the dike was fixed, they hoisted him onto their shoulders and carried him to town as a hero. To this day, people still tell the story of Hans, the boy who saved Harlem.

Finding Imagery

After reading "The Hero of Harlem" (page 16), answer the questions.

1. Summarize the story in one sentence. Your summary should include the main characters, the conflict, and the resolution.

   _____

   _____

2. Using the image and the text, tell what a *dike* is.

   _____

   _____

3. Without the image, would you have known what a *dike* is? Explain.

   _____

   _____

4. Circle the sentence that best describes the theme of the story.
   A. Water can be a destructive force.
   B. Never give up. No one is too small to make a difference.
   C. Being a hero is an important goal.
   D. Brothers should stick together.

5. *Personification* is a literary technique used to give human qualities to a nonliving thing. Write an example of personification used in this story.

   _____

   _____

Helping at Home Ask your child to read aloud the words spoken in the story by the voice of the ocean. Why does the author give the ocean a voice? Ask your child to imagine that the dike in the story has a voice, too. What would the dike say to the ocean? To Hans?

Characters, Settings, and Events

Read the story.

The Yew Tree
by Ruedigar Matthes (adapted)

Long ago in Scotland, Finlay, a 12-year-old boy with messy red hair, was walking along the river's edge. Finlay was a good boy with a good heart, but he had had a hard life and little good fortune. As an orphan, Finlay had lived with many different uncles and aunts, none of whom had really welcomed him, and he never stayed long in one place. But, Finlay's misfortune was about to change.

As Finlay walked by the river's edge on this particular day, he slipped on a mossy rock and fell headlong into the frigid water. He landed with a splash, hitting his head on a rock. Finlay's mind went blank as the swift current carried him away.

Finlay woke to a small lamb licking his face. He pushed away the lamb, sat up, and rubbed his throbbing head. Finlay looked around the small room and tried to figure out where he was, but he had never seen the green, sheep-covered hills that surrounded the cottage he was in.

"Hello, lad," a warm, booming voice said. "You should be careful, for your head has a large bump, as well as a cut. When I found you, you were soaked from head to toe, lying in a pile of mossy wood on the riverbank."

"I don't really remember what happened. Where am I? And, who are you?"

"I am a shepherd called Murchadh. Who are you?"

"I am called Finlay."

"Well, perhaps you would like a nice bowl of mutton stew?"

"I am starving, and so I will accept your offer of stew, good sir." Finlay ate as if he had not eaten for days. When he was finished, he pushed away the bowl.

Murchadh looked outside and began to speak. "It will be dark soon. You should spend the night here. My home is small, but it has served me well for many years."

"Thank you for everything," Finlay said. "But, I must be home before it gets dark. My uncle will be furious if I am late. Thank you again." He stood up and hastily headed out the door.

(to be continued . . .)

Characters, Settings, and Events

After reading "The Yew Tree" (page 18), answer the questions.

1. Describe the characters Finlay and Murchadh. How are they alike? How are they different? Use details from the story to support your answer.

_____

_____

_____

2. Contrast Finlay's home life with Murchadh's home life. Use details from the story to support your answer.

_____

_____

_____

3. Circle the time setting that best describes when this story took place. Use details from the story to support your answer.
   A. present day
   B. about a hundred years ago
   C. thousands of years ago
   D. millions of years ago

_____

_____

4. Cite evidence from the story that supports the idea that "Finlay's misfortune was about to change."

_____

_____

© Carson-Dellosa • CD-704505

Helping at Home

Have fun with your child telling silly stories that result from mixing up familiar characters, settings, and events. What might happen if Harry Potter visited the land of Oz? What if Laura Ingalls found the ring from *The Lord of the Rings*?

Comparing Stories

Read the story.

The Yew Tree
by Ruedigar Matthes (adapted)
(continued from page 18)

After leaving Murchadh's house, Finlay followed a small trail that cut through the hillside. The sun lowered slowly behind the horizon like the curtain at the end of a play. Suddenly, a hungry fox came out of nowhere and startled Finlay. Without thinking, Finlay turned and ran toward Murchadh's home with the fox on his heels. As he grew tired of running, Finlay stopped and climbed the closest tree—a dead yew tree. The fox paced around the foot of the tree for a few minutes and then turned and jogged away. Just to be sure that he had escaped the fox, Finlay decided to stay in the tree for a while. Soon, he fell asleep to the soft gurgling of a nearby stream.

While he slept, Finlay dreamed that the yew tree curled around his body and kept him warm. He dreamt of a voice whispering the secret to finding good fortune. When he awoke, Finlay looked around. The world seemed different—the sun shone brightly, and the sky was a brilliant blue. Finlay wanted to stay under that sky forever. He decided that he would go back to Murchadh's house and live with him. He climbed down from the tangled branches of the tree and ran toward Murchadh's house.

On his way, Finlay became thirsty and knelt to drink from the nearby stream. After quenching his thirst, he noticed a strange, bright rock. He plucked it from the stream, placed it in his pocket, and continued walking down the path. When he spotted Murchadh's house, he ran as fast as could and burst breathlessly through the door.

"I want to stay and live with you," Finlay blurted out. "I will be a shepherd, and I will work very hard. I promise." He told Murchadh all about his night in the yew. When Finlay finished his story, Murchadh said, "There is a legend about a man who climbed the branches of a yew tree and never came down. According to the legend, if you climb the yew tree and stay awhile, the man will whisper in your ear the way to go to find good fortune. Maybe the yew tree told you to come help a poor shepherd who is getting too old to tend his sheep."

As Finlay embraced the old man, the rock he had found in the stream earlier fell from his pocket. "I found this unusual rock," he said.

"My goodness, lad, this is gold! The voice in the yew tree did tell you where to find fortune!" For the first time in as long as he could remember, Finlay felt fortunate.

Comparing Stories

After reading "The Hero of Harlem" (page 16) and "The Yew Tree" (pages 18 and 20), answer the questions, comparing the two stories.

1. Summarize the story "The Yew Tree." Your summary should include the main characters, the conflict, and the resolution.

   _____

   _____

2. Circle the sentence that best describes the theme of "The Yew Tree."
   A. Good fortune comes to good people.
   B. Trees bring good luck.
   C. Shepherds care for sheep and children.
   D. Good fortune only happens in stories.

3. The stories "The Hero of Harlem" and "The Yew Tree" are both folktales. Complete the graphic organizer to compare and contrast the two stories.

Folktale Characteristics	"The Hero of Harlem"	"The Yew Tree"
Ordinary Characters		
Storyteller's Beginning		
A Problem to Solve		
A Happy Ending		
A Positive Theme		

Helping at Home

Ask your child to think of a familiar folktale such as "Stone Soup" or "The Legend of Excalibur." Can your child use details from that story to fill in a fourth column for the chart on this page? What other characteristics do all three stories have in common?

Metaphors and Similes

Circle the two words or phrases that are being compared in each sentence. Then, write a sentence to explain the comparison.

1. The row of trees looked like soldiers standing at attention.

   _____

2. Looking down from the airplane, the cars were ants crawling along the highway.

   _____

3. Twenty circus clowns packed into one little car as sardines are packed in a can.

   _____

4. The shadows were ghosts dancing on the sunlit lawn.

   _____

5. The sound of waves lapping the shore reminded me of a dog getting a long drink.

   _____

6. The baseball flew like a rocket out of the ballpark.

   _____

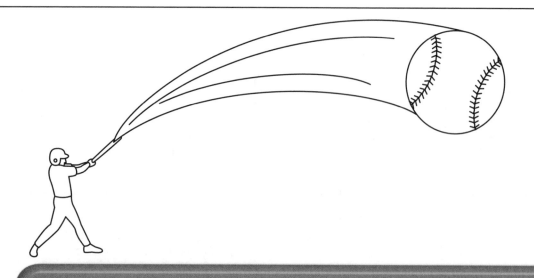

Helping
at Home

Metaphors and similes compare two unlike things. Comparisons can be beautiful, vivid, and fun. Have fun with your child thinking of silly, dramatic similes and metaphors to describe everyday activities such as putting on socks or loading the dishwasher.

Main Idea and Details

Read the passage. Then, answer the questions.

Laws to Live By

Laws are rules that we live by every day. Imagine if drivers paid no attention to stoplights, if pedestrians crossed roads wherever and whenever they wanted, or if speed limits did not exist. Traffic laws maintain safety and also protect the rights of others.

Laws are enforced by the police and interpreted by the courts. Police officers make sure that the laws are obeyed, and courts enforce the laws. Judges in the courts make sure that laws are carried out fairly and "according to the law."

Courts in the United States have three responsibilities. First, they interpret the laws and make sure that they are followed by everyone. Second, the courts determine punishment for those who are found guilty of breaking the laws. Finally, they must protect the rights of every individual.

Laws can be changed to meet the needs of a nation. Although laws have changed over the years, the principles that govern the judicial system have not. These principles ensure that everyone is protected equally under the law and has a right to a fair trial with a fitting punishment for a crime. But, most important, these principles guarantee that every citizen has the right to practice the many freedoms specified in the U.S. Constitution.

1. What is the main idea of the passage?

_____

_____

2. List three ideas that support the main idea.

_____

_____

_____

3. Why do we have laws?

_____

_____

Helping at Home

Encourage your child to read a newspaper, magazine, or online article about a topic that he or she finds interesting. Ask your child to share three details from the article. Then ask, "What main idea do those details support?"

Finding Evidence

Read the story.

Maria Sklodowska

Have you heard of Maria Sklodowska? Probably not. But, you may have heard of Marie Curie. This is a real-life story of how a poor, young Polish girl grew up to become a world-famous scientist.

Maria Sklodowska was born on November 7, 1867, in Warsaw, Poland. She grew up in an area of Poland where learning was considered a privilege. Her father was a professor. Although she grew up without much money, she was surrounded by science equipment. In 1891, she went to Paris, France, to go to college. While in France, she began to use the French spelling of her first name, Marie.

Sklodowska received her physics degree in 1893, graduating first in her class. In 1894, she earned a mathematics degree, graduating second in her class. She met a scientist named Pierre Curie. They were married in 1895. The husband-and-wife team became known worldwide for their work. They studied radioactivity. The Curies made many new discoveries. Marie Curie was awarded the Nobel Prize. She later became the first female professor at the university in Paris.

She died on July 4, 1934, of a disease caused by her work with radioactive materials.

Finding Evidence

After reading "Maria Sklodowska" (page 24), follow the directions.

1. Is the passage fiction or nonfiction? Write evidence from the text that supports your answer.

   _____

   _____

2. Write two accomplishments of Maria Sklodowska that provide evidence that she became a world-famous scientist.

   _____

   _____

3. Circle the statement you can infer from "learning was considered a privilege."
   A. Everyone went to school.
   B. Only the rich went to school.

4. Create a time line of Maria Sklodowska's life.

Helping at Home

Have your child ask several questions about Marie Curie that are not answered in the passage. Encourage him or her to do research to discover the answers and to add more dates to the time line. Can your child summarize the life of Marie Curie?

Connecting Ideas

Read the passage.

Louis Pasteur

Louis Pasteur was a famous scientist. He was born in France in 1822. Pasteur earned a degree as a doctor of science, but he was not a physician. Because he was not a medical doctor, many members of the medical profession did not take his work seriously. Pasteur, however, believed strongly that germs existed and that they caused disease. He discovered a way to control the spread of a silkworm disease. He also developed vaccines for rabies and anthrax. Pasteur made great strides in the medical field.

Pasteur also developed a process to keep milk free of germs. The process involves heating the milk to 140°F (60°C) for 30 minutes. The milk is then cooled quickly and sealed in sterile containers. This process is called pasteurization. Each time you drink a glass of cold milk, you have Pasteur to thank.

In his later years, the medical community recognized the importance of Pasteur's work. In 1888, Pasteur opened a research center in Paris, France. It is called the Pasteur Institute. Pasteur directed the work that was done there until his death in 1895. Today, more than 100 years later, scientists at the institute continue to build on his ideas.

Connecting Ideas

After reading "Maria Sklodowska" (page 24) and "Louis Pasteur" (page 26), follow the directions.

1. What evidence from the passage supports the statement, "Louis Pasteur was a famous scientist"?

   _____

   _____

   _____

2. What is a *physician*? _____

3. What does it mean that "Pasteur earned a degree as a doctor of science, but he was not a physician"?

   _____

   _____

4. Do you think that Louis Pasteur and Maria Sklodowska knew of each other's work? Use evidence from the passages to support your answer.

   _____

   _____

5. Draw a time line of Louis Pasteur's life. Add the dates of Maria Sklodowska's birth and death to the time line.

Helping at Home

Louis Pasteur and Marie Curie lived during the late nineteenth century. Ask your child to read a book or Web site to learn about another scientific discovery made during this time period. Ask your child to add it to the time line on this page.

Using Information from Reading

Read the passage.

A Pioneer of Flight

A Budding Interest

Amelia Earhart saw an airplane for the first time at a state fair in 1907. She was 10 years old. Not until a decade later, while attending a stunt-flying exhibition, did she really become interested in flying.

A Rise to Fame

As a social worker, Earhart had never had any experience with airplanes. Determined to learn how to fly, she took her first lesson in 1921. In just six months, she saved enough money to buy her own airplane. It was bright yellow. She named it Canary. She set her first record in it. She became the first woman to fly up to 14,000 feet (4267 m).

Earhart flew often. Her hard work paid off in 1928 when a book publisher named George P. Putnam asked her if she would fly across the Atlantic Ocean. Her answer was yes. She became a celebrity. From that point on, Earhart's life centered on flying. She became popular as she won competitions and awards.

Earhart married George Putnam in 1931. Together, they planned her solo trek across the Atlantic Ocean in 1932. When she returned home, President Herbert Hoover awarded her a medal. More medals followed. In 1935, she became the first person to fly solo from Hawaii to California.

A Mysterious End

Earhart set a new goal. She wanted to be the first woman to fly around the world. Despite a failed first attempt, Earhart departed from Florida in 1937. Navigator Fred Noonan flew with her. During this flight, they disappeared. Earhart tried to land on a small island in the Pacific Ocean. She missed the island because of cloudy conditions. Her airplane never landed. A rescue attempt began immediately. They never found Earhart or her airplane, but she lives on as a legend in aviation history.

Using Information from Reading

After reading "A Pioneer of Flight" (page 28), follow the directions.

1. Make a time line of the events that led Amelia Earhart to become an aviator.

2. Write a newspaper article that reports Amelia Earhart's disappearance. Use the five Ws: *who, what, when, why,* and *where.*

_____

_____

_____

_____

_____

_____

3. Since 1937, people have searched unsuccessfully for Amelia Earhart's airplane. There are many theories about what happened. What do you think happened to Amelia Earhart? Use evidence from the text to support your thinking.

_____

_____

_____

Helping at Home

As your child completes item #2 on this page, ask him or her to underline each question word (*who, what,* etc.) with a different colored pencil. Then, have your child underline information from the passage that answers the question with the matching colored pencil.

Organizing Information

Read the passage.

John Colter: Western Explorer

A Wilderness Traveler

John Colter explored more of the American wilderness than nearly any explorer of his time. He was one of the first settlers to cross North America and see the Pacific Ocean. He traveled through the American Indian territories. He saw amazing natural wonders.

Exploring

In 1804, Colter set off into the unknown wilderness of the American West. He traveled with a group called the Corps of Discovery. Lewis and Clark led the group. The Corps included 32 men, a young American Indian woman named Sacagawea, and her baby. The goal was to find a waterway that connected the Missouri River and the Pacific Ocean. The corps members suffered hardship, hunger, sickness, and fatigue.

Fur Trapping

After nearly two years in the wilderness, the Corps of Discovery was headed back to St. Louis, Missouri. They met a company of fur trappers coming up the Missouri River. The company was eager to gain information about the wilderness, so Colter decided to join them and be their guide. On one of his trips, Colter came across a strange landscape. Water boiled from the earth and shot 70 feet (21 m) into the air. Thick mud bubbled from stinking pools and filled the air with a foul stench. All kinds of wild animals roamed freely through this land of beauty. Today, we call the area Yellowstone National Park.

John Colter lived a life of adventure. But, how did he die? No one knows for sure, but many historians believe that his death was neither violent nor heroic. According to some accounts, Colter died at home in his bed.

Organizing Information

After reading "A Pioneer of Flight" (page 28) and "John Colter: Western Explorer" (page 30), answer the questions.

1. What is John Colter famous for? Use evidence from the passage to support your answer.

_____

_____

_____

2. What are some similarities between John Colter and Amelia Earhart?

_____

_____

_____

3. Compare the organization of "A Pioneer of Flight" and "John Colter: Western Explorer." How are they alike?

_____

_____

_____

4. Contrast the organization of "A Pioneer of Flight" and "John Colter: Western Explorer." How are they different?

_____

_____

_____

Helping at Home

Talk about ways to organize information. Brainstorm facts that could be organized by time order (example: a weekly menu), by cause/effect (example: science experiments), by events or categories (example: famous accomplishments), etc.

Using Information from Reading

Read the passage.

John Colter's Escape

John Colter became a legend of the great expansion. One story is told about how he escaped from a tribe of American Indians. Members of the Blackfoot tribe captured him and his traveling companion, John Potts. Potts was shot, and Colter was taken back to their camp. They took his clothes and his shoes. They held a council to decide his fate. Colter could understand some of their language, and he heard them discussing how to do away with him.

The chief told Colter to start walking away from the camp. After he had walked a few hundred yards, someone yelled. All of the braves in the camp sprinted after him. The Yellowstone River was five miles away. Colter knew that if he could get to the river, he might have a chance of escaping the tribe. The ground was rough and covered with sharp rocks and prickly pear cacti. The braves wore thick moccasins. Colter raced for his life on bare feet. The soles of his feet were soon covered with cactus needles. Several braves were gaining on him. He could have given up, but his will to live roared like a great fire within him. He pushed himself to run faster.

He called upon every bit of strength and energy he had in his body. After a couple of miles, his nose started to bleed. At last, he reached the river and dove in. The icy water washed away the blood and soothed his torn feet. He hid in the river as the braves searched for him. He stayed in the river until dark. Then, he crawled out to finish his escape. He climbed a mountain in the dark and finally stumbled into a trading post a few weeks later.

Although John Colter blazed trails with Lewis and Clark, explored a vast wilderness, and discovered fabulous geysers, his greatest discovery was learning how strong his will to live could be.

Using Information from Reading

After reading "John Colter: Western Explorer" (page 30) and "John Colter's Escape" (page 32), use the graphic organizer to plan information for a brief report about John Colter. Then, write the report on another sheet of paper or on a computer.

Title:
Introductory Sentence Stating Main Idea:
Supporting Detail or Fact from the Passages:
Supporting Detail or Fact from the Passages:
Supporting Detail or Fact from the Passages:
Concluding Sentence Summarizing the Main Idea:

Helping at Home

Help your child select a main idea for the report on this page by asking what he or she finds most interesting about John Colter. His sense of adventure? His encounters with American Indians? What information from the passages relates to this idea?

Main Idea

Read the passage.

Immigration at Angel Island

In 1882, Congress passed a law called the Chinese Exclusion Act. It was passed to keep Chinese people from *immigrating* to America. Chinese workers had come to the United States to work as *merchants* or in mines. They helped build railroads. But, some Americans were afraid that Chinese people would take their jobs. The law made it hard for Chinese people to enter the country. It said that only the relatives of citizens would be allowed in. No other people faced such *discrimination*.

At that time, there was a large section of San Francisco, California, called Chinatown. Thousands of Chinese people went there. In 1906, San Francisco had a large earthquake. A fire started because of the earthquake. The fire destroyed much of the city. When Chinatown burned, so did many records of *citizenship*. The government did not know which Chinese people coming to America were related to citizens. The people who were related to citizens would be able to stay. The other people would have to return to China.

In 1910, the government opened a station for immigrants. The station was built on Angel Island in San Francisco's *harbor*. Each Chinese immigrant had to wait there until he could prove that he had a relative who was a citizen. The average Chinese immigrant was *detained* on the island for two to three weeks. However, some people spent months or even years at the Immigration Station. Some Chinese immigrants told stories of their experiences through poetry that they carved on the walls of the wooden *barracks* where they lived.

The Chinese Exclusion Act was *repealed* in 1943. More than 250,000 Chinese immigrants came through Angel Island. Today, it is a state park with bike trails, hiking trails, camping spots, and boats. The barracks where immigrants lived are a historic site. The poetry they carved there has been translated into English.

Main Idea

After reading "Immigration at Angel Island" (page 34), answer the questions.

1. What is the main idea of the passage?

_____

_____

_____

_____

Match each word with its definition.

2. _____ unfair treatment of a group of people   A. barracks

3. _____ people who buy and sell goods   B. detained

4. _____ a place along the ocean where ships dock   C. discrimination

5. _____ membership in a country   D. immigrating

6. _____ canceled or withdrawn   E. harbor

7. _____ coming to a country from another one   F. citizenship

8. _____ temporary buildings that house many people   G. merchants

9. _____ held   H. repealed

Helping at Home
Ask your child whether the passage is fiction or nonfiction. Does the author state an opinion, or are all the statements facts? Challenge your child to summarize the passage using only factual statements.

Comparing Texts

Read the play.

Poems from Angel Island

Tour Guide: Welcome to the Angel Island Immigration Station. Surrounding you in these barracks are records of the people who stayed here from 1910 to 1940. What do you see on this wall?

Student 1: Writing has been carved into the wood, and it is in another language.

Tour Guide: The language is Chinese. Our translators, Lin and Hai, will help us read what it says.

Lin: This part says, "I took a raft and sailed the seas. Rising early at dawn with the stars above my head. Traveling deep into the night, the moon my companion."

Hai: "Who knew my trip would be full of rain and snow?"

Tour Guide: Many Chinese people left their homes and sailed to America. When they got here, they had to wait to become citizens. They were detained in these small wooden barracks.

Student 2: Why did they write on the walls?

Tour Guide: Imagine you were forced to live in a place such as this. How would you feel?

Student 2: I would feel angry or maybe sad.

Tour Guide: Other poems carved into the walls tell us more about how the Chinese people felt.

Lin: Here, it says, "I have walked to the very edge of the earth. A dusty, windy journey. I am worn out. Who can save me? I am like a fish out of water."

Hai: "I worry for my parents, my wife, and my son. Do they have enough firewood and food?"

Lin: "We are kept in a dark, filthy room. Who would have thought that my joy would turn into sorrow?"

Hai: "Cruel treatment, not one breath of fresh air. Little food, many restrictions. Here, even a proud man bows his head low."

Tour Guide: Thanks, Lin and Hai, for translating today. We can learn from mistakes by studying history. The words carved into this wall are preserved so that we remember the past.

Comparing Texts

After reading "Immigration at Angel Island" (page 34) and "Poems from Angel Island" (page 36), answer the questions.

1. What is the topic of both "Immigration at Angel Island" and "Poems from Angel Island"?

_____

_____

2. What is the purpose of both "Immigration at Angel Island" and "Poems from Angel Island"?

_____

_____

3. What information is provided in both "Immigration at Angel Island" and "Poems from Angel Island"?

_____

_____

4. What information is provided in "Immigration at Angel Island" but not in "Poems from Angel Island"?

_____

_____

5. What information is provided in "Poems from Angel Island" but not in "Immigration at Angel Island"?

_____

_____

Helping at Home

Share with your child memories about an eventful time in history that you lived through. Then, ask your child to read a book or Web site about that time. Ask your child to compare and contrast information from the reading with the story you told.

Writing an Opinion

Write an essay to support an opinion you have. Use the graphic organizer to help you state your opinion and organize the reasons that support your opinion.

What is your opinion on the topic?

_____

_____

_____

_____

_____

_____

_____

_____

Whom are you trying to persuade?

_____

_____

_____

_____

_____

_____

_____

_____

List three reasons to support your opinion.

_____

_____

_____

To convince the reader, add supporting facts and details for each reason.

_____

_____

_____

Help your child brainstorm topics for an opinion essay. Include issues about which fifth graders and adults might disagree, such as privileges at home or at school. Help your child clearly state his or her opinion about each issue.

Writing an Opinion

Use the following format to organize the first draft of your opinion essay (page 38). Use words and phrases to connect your opinion to your reasons.

also	another	because	consequently	for example
in addition to	since	specifically	such as	therefore

Paragraph 1: State your opinion and the three reasons that support your opinion.

_____

_____

_____

Paragraph 2: State your first reason and explain the reason providing facts and details.

_____

_____

_____

Paragraph 3: State your second reason and explain the reason providing facts and details.

_____

_____

_____

Paragraph 4: State your third reason and explain the reason providing facts and details.

_____

_____

_____

Paragraph 5: Write a conclusion restating your opinion and restating the reasons.

_____

_____

_____

Helping at Home

Talk with your child about what it means to be a *devil's advocate* and intentionally argue against an opinion you support. How can playing devil's advocate help your child think of good reasons, facts, and details to support his or her actual opinion?

Revising and Editing

Use the editing checklist to produce a final copy of your opinion essay (pages 38 and 39). Type your final draft on a computer or write it on another sheet of paper. Attach your first draft and this editing sheet to your final draft. Then, have another person read your essay and complete the bottom part of this sheet.

Plan

_____ I have made a written plan that outlines my opinion, my audience, the reasons for my opinion, and facts and details that support the reasons.

Revise

_____ I have written an introductory paragraph that states my opinion.

_____ I have written a closing paragraph that summarizes my opinion.

_____ I have revised my writing for clarity.

_____ I have used transition words and phrases to connect ideas.

Edit

_____ I have used words correctly.

_____ I have written complete sentences.

_____ I have edited my writing for capitalization and punctuation.

_____ I have edited my writing for spelling errors.

Publish

_____ I have asked someone to read my essay.

The following is to be completed by the reader:

I have read this essay. (signature)_____

I agree / disagree (circle one) with the opinion in this essay because

_____

_____

Ask your child to use markers or colored pencils to rewrite the checklist items from this page on the inside of a file folder or on a bookmark cut from construction paper. Encourage your child to keep the checklist handy for future revising and editing.

Writing to Inform

Prepare to write a report about something you are studying at school in science or social studies. Use the graphic organizer to help you plan and organize your writing.

Topic

Subtopic 1	Subtopic 2	Subtopic 3

Special Topic Key Words	Special Text Features (maps, charts, etc.)

Finding a report topic that is not too broad or too narrow can be a challenge. Choose a broad topic such as *the ocean*. Ask your child to think of more focused topics that relate to the ocean. Talk about which would make good topics for a research report.

Taking Notes

Before writing your report (page 41), research information about the topic. Use a book, the Internet, or other reference materials to gather information. Take notes on your topic.

Topic:

Subtopic 1: Fact: Fact: Source:
Subtopic 2: Fact: Fact: Source:
Subtopic 3: Fact: Fact: Source:

Helping at Home

Talk with your child about reliable sources, including firsthand accounts, books, and Web sites that are updated and maintained by experts. Do an Internet search on your child's report topic and help him or her pick out the most reliable information.

Writing to Inform

Use the following format to organize the first draft of your research report (pages 41 and 42). Use words and phrases to connect the ideas throughout your report.

Title: _____

Introductory Paragraph: State your topic, why you chose the topic, and general information about the topic.

_____

_____

Subtopic 1 Heading: _____
State the main idea of subtopic 1 and at least three supporting details.

_____

_____

Subtopic 2 Heading: _____
State the main idea of subtopic 2 and at least three supporting details.

_____

_____

Subtopic 3 Heading: _____
State the main idea of subtopic 3 and at least three supporting details.

_____

_____

Concluding Paragraph: Summarize the information from the report.

_____

_____

Transitional Words

Read the paragraph. Write time-order words or phrases on the lines to help the events of the passage flow. You can use the time-order words from the list or write your own. Be sure to include commas as necessary.

at last	at this point	finally	first	in conclusion
in the meantime	meanwhile	next	then	

Growing a Sunflower

Did you know that you can plant a sunflower seed inside a cup? It is simple and fun!

_____ gather the following materials: a clear, plastic cup; a wet paper

towel; and a sunflower seed. _____ place the paper towel inside the cup.

_____ make sure that the paper towel covers the entire inside of the cup. Place

the seed on the paper towel and fold the paper towel over the

seed. _____ place the cup near a window with a lot

of sunlight shining through. If your sunflower does not get enough

sunlight, it will not be able to grow. It will take three weeks for your

seed to sprout. _____ you can record any changes

that you observe. _____ you will be able to see

your sunflower flourish.

© Carson-Dellosa • CD-704505

Helping at Home

Ask your child to tell you a story about something that happened at school. Touch your nose (or make another gesture) each time your child uses a transitional word. Next, tell your own story and have your child note your transitional words.

Developing Characters

Many authors create characters based on people they know in real life. Think about someone who is special to you such as a parent, a brother or sister, or a friend. Draw the person's face in the middle of this page. Then, answer the questions.

What does the character look like?

_____

_____

_____

What does the character think?

_____

_____

_____

How does the character act?

_____

_____

_____

What is the character's name?

_____

_____

_____

Helping at Home

Have fun with your child inventing a fictional family member. What is the person's name? What does he or she like to do, wear, eat, watch on TV, etc.? What kinds of adventures and misadventures might the character have as a family member?

Developing Settings

Use the five senses to describe each setting. Include vivid details in your descriptions.

1. The attic of a house in the winter

_____

_____

_____

2. A lighthouse near the ocean

_____

_____

_____

3. A flower garden in a park

_____

_____

_____

4. A crowded elevator

_____

_____

_____

Helping at Home

Think of a place you and your child know well. It could be a vacation spot, a nearby park, or a grandparent's house. Together, think of 15 vivid words and phrases to describe the place. What kind of story might happen there?

Writing a Story

Write a story. Use the flowchart to help you plan your story.

Setting: _____

↓

Characters: _____

↓

Problem: _____
_____

Event 1: _____
_____
_____
_____
_____
_____
_____

→

Event 2: _____
_____
_____
_____
_____
_____
_____

→

Event 3: _____
_____
_____
_____
_____
_____
_____

Solution: _____
_____

Helping at Home

Provide a blank notebook. Encourage your child to use it for writing a complete copy of the story including illustrations. Over time, encourage your child to fill up the notebook by writing more installments of the story.

Writing About Literature

To become a better writer, it is important to read. Read "The Hero of Harlem" (page 16). Use the flowchart to help you recognize the strategies the author of this story used.

Setting: _____

Characters: _____

Problem: _____
_____

Event 1: _____
_____
_____
_____
_____
_____
_____

Event 2: _____
_____
_____
_____
_____
_____
_____

Event 3: _____
_____
_____
_____
_____
_____
_____

Solution: _____
_____

Helping at Home

Talk about a *story arc*, or typical story pattern in which a problem is introduced, builds to a climax, and then resolves. Challenge your child to describe the story pattern of a favorite book, movie, or TV episode.

Conjunctions

Use a conjunction from the word bank to combine each pair of simple sentences. Then, write the new sentences. You may use a conjunction more than once.

although	and	because	but	or	so	while

1. Sarah wanted to go swimming. It rained. _____

_____

2. The car broke down. I took a taxi. _____

_____

3. The man was tired. The man sat on a bench. _____

_____

4. It started raining. I opened my umbrella. _____

_____

5. I watered the plant. It wilted. _____

_____

6. The baby cried. The baby was hungry. _____

_____

7. Jeremy bought some milk. He still had some left. _____

_____

8. The boy started a new painting. His first painting was drying. _____

_____

Teach your child the mnemonic phrase *FAN BOYS* to help remember the coordinating conjunctions that can join two sentences. They are *for, and, nor, but, or, yet,* and *so.* Coordinating conjunctions should always be preceded by a comma.

Interjections

Underline the interjection in each sentence.

1. Well, we are learning about Egyptian pyramids.

2. Wow, the first pyramid was built in 2780 BC.

3. Yes, we read about the Great Pyramid at Giza.

4. Phew, the Great Pyramid spans 13 acres of land!

5. No, I didn't know that it stands near the Sphinx.

Complete each sentence using an interjection from the word bank. Be sure to include commas as necessary.

Great	Hey	Wait	Wow	Yes

6. _____ our room looks like ancient Egypt!

7. _____ we decorated the room for our Egyptian feast.

8. _____ Anna forgot the grapes.

9. _____ I have some we can use.

10. _____ we can use those for our feast.

Helping at Home Talk with your child about how some interjections such as *oh*, *ouch*, *ah*, and *uh-huh*, are examples of onomatopoeia, or words that name sounds. When a strong feeling is expressed, an interjection may be followed by an exclamation mark: *Ouch! That hurt.*

Prepositions

Underline the preposition in each sentence.

1. The sun shines in our universe.

2. Many planets revolve around the sun.

3. Our planet has one moon in its orbit.

4. The moon orbits near Earth.

5. The *Phoenix* landed on Mars.

6. Sometimes, you can see Venus at night.

7. Jupiter is the largest planet in the solar system.

8. Mercury is the closest planet to our sun.

Insert commas as needed. Then, underline the conjunctions. Not every sentence has a conjunction.

9. Wow there is a lot to learn about the solar system.

10. Our group made models of Mars Earth and Venus.

11. Oh no our models of Earth and Venus fell apart but the model of Mars is fine.

12. Jeremy would you like to travel to Mars or Venus some day?

13. The planets moons and stars are part of the solar system.

14. Don't you think this has been an interesting unit Robert?

Helping at Home

A prepositional phrase can be short (example: *over there*) or longer (*under the warm, fuzzy blanket*). It is never part of the subject of a sentence. Ask your child to read a page from a chapter book and identify five prepositional phrases.

Perfect Tense

Write the perfect tense of each verb.

	Present Perfect	Past Perfect	Future Perfect
1. walk	_____	_____	_____
2. run	_____	_____	_____
3. jump	_____	_____	_____
4. skip	_____	_____	_____
5. hop	_____	_____	_____
6. join	_____	_____	_____

Complete each sentence with the correct perfect tense of the verb in parentheses.

7. By Friday, the dancers _____ the difficult dance steps. (learn)

8. The dancers _____ difficult dance steps for many performances. (learn)

9. The dancers _____ difficult dance steps before these steps. (learn)

Using Verb Tenses

Circle the incorrect verb in each sentence. Rewrite the sentence using the correct verb tense.

1. Scientists have learn that rhinoceroses have lived on Earth for about 40 million years.

_____

2. Fossils showing that there were more than 30 species of rhinos.

_____

3. A rhinoceros ranking as one of the largest land creatures.

_____

4. Most wild rhinos will live in Africa, southeastern Asia, and Sumatra.

_____

5. Indian rhinos had skin that looks like a suit of armor.

_____

6. They inhabiting marshy jungles among reeds and tall grasses.

_____

7. Illegal hunters, called poachers, have hunt rhinos for their valuable horns for many years.

_____

8. Some people grinds up rhino horns to treat sicknesses.

_____

Send your child a text message or e-mail message that includes several incorrect shifts in verb tense (example: *How were you? I hoping you are well. Would you have liked tacos for dinner?*). Let your child correct the message and send it back to you.

Correlative Conjunctions

Complete each sentence with a correlative conjunction (either/or, neither/nor, both/and).

1. _____ James _____ Ryan like the Red Sox baseball team.

2. _____ James _____ Ryan play for the White Sox.

3. James _____ plays first base, _____ he plays outfield.

4. _____ James _____ Ryan got up to bat in the first inning.

5. Unfortunately, _____ James _____ Ryan got a hit.

6. However, in the third inning, _____ James _____ Ryan got hits.

7. _____ Ryan _____ James will sit out the fourth inning to let Sam play.

8. _____ Ryan _____ James like sitting out.

9. _____ James _____ Ryan like to win.

10. After the game, the team will celebrate by going out for _____ pizza

_____ burgers.

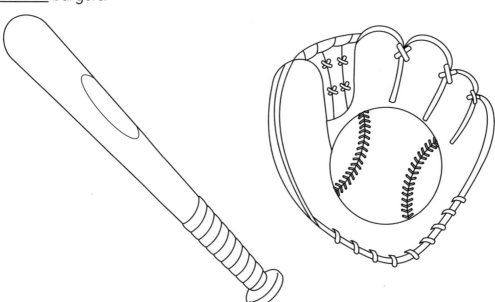

Have your child search for and read the poem "Who Has Seen the Wind?" by Christina Rossetti. Does it use *neither/nor* correctly? Could *either/or* and *both/and* be substituted for those words? How would they change the poem's meaning?

Words in a Series

Rewrite each sentence, inserting commas to separate items in a series.

1. Hayden ordered lasagna salad and milk for dinner.

_____

2. Hayden likes zucchini, but he does not like beans peas or spinach.

_____

3. Hayden couldn't decide whether to have the chocolate strawberry or vanilla yogurt for dessert.

_____

4. Peaches pears and grapes are my favorite fruits.

_____

5. Which do you like most, peaches pears or grapes?

_____

6. My mother made a fruit salad with apples bananas strawberries and grapes.

_____

7. Nicole Marisa and I enjoyed eating the fruit salad.

_____

Helping at Home

Have your child search a newspaper and a chapter book for examples of words in a series. Is a comma used after each word, including before *and* or *or*? Explain that in writing done for school, there should always be a comma before *and* or *or* in a series.

Commas: Introductory Elements and Direct Address

Rewrite each sentence, inserting commas to set off an introductory phrase or to indicate direct address.

1. Because my dad was a Boy Scout our family lives by the motto, "Be prepared."

   _____

2. Until my sister is a little older my parents will not take us to the amusement park.

   _____

3. Before we leave to go anywhere we lock the door to our house.

   _____

4. After hearing about the fire at our neighbor's house my family made an emergency plan.

   _____

5. Because my cousin is allergic to peanuts we cannot have peanuts in our home.

   _____

6. Yes my family must arrive at the airport at least two hours before our flight leaves.

   _____

7. Although I think my family is a bit too cautious I appreciate the care they have for me.

   _____

8. Is your family as cautious as my family Claire?

   _____

9. Jose you will have to leave by seven o'clock.

   _____

Take turns with your child reading several sentences from this page aloud. Can you hear the pause where the comma should be?

Writing Titles

Write each story title correctly.

1. The Ugly Duckling _____

2. The Lion's Share _____

3. The Fir Tree _____

Write each poem title correctly.

4. Shooting Stars _____

5. Always Wondering _____

6. Floradora Doe _____

Write each song title correctly.

7. Down in the Valley _____

8. Go Tell Aunt Rhody _____

9. Monster Mash _____

Rewrite each sentence, correctly punctuating the titles of works.

10. Our class read the story The Golden Touch.

_____

11. We sang the Star Spangled Banner at the baseball game.

_____

12. I memorized the entire poem Paul Revere's Ride.

_____

Helping at Home

Explain that books or music albums often contain many stories, poems, or songs. Book and album names are underlined or shown in italics (example: *A Fairy Tale Collection*), while included titles are shown in quotation marks ("The Ugly Duckling").

Spelling

Cross out each misspelled word. Then, write the word correctly above the misspelled word. Use a dictionary if needed. There are 12 misspelled words.

Best Friends

Kelly, Aaron, Brandon, and I are best freinds. We are in the same class at school. We have so much fun when we are together. We wanted to go to the movies, so we asked our parents. After our parents agreed to take us, we decided on a movie and made plans to meet at the theater Saturday afternoon. Kelly arrived first, and Aaron and Brandon arrived imediatly after. As usual, I was late. By the time I got their, every one was in line to buy snacks. They knew better than to wait for me. Brandon ordered nachos, popcorn, and a large lemonade. I could not beleive that he planned to eat so much. "I'm a growing boy," Brandon always said. The rest of us decided to share a large pop corn. Then, it was time to find our seats. The theater was so dark we couldn't see any thing. We stumbled in and sat in the first row. Luckily, the theater was empty becuz we spent the entire time whispering and giggleing. I could not even tell you what the movie was about. After it ended, our parents picked us up. We said goodby and headed home. If our parents agree, we will get together agin next weekend and go bowling. Its fun to have best friends.

Provide a little notebook where your child can keep an alphabetized list of "spelling demons," or words that are especially difficult to spell correctly. He or she might begin with these tricky words: *cupboard, often, receive, straight, tomorrow.*

Using Adjectives and Adverbs

Write the adjective or adverb in parentheses that makes each sentence clearer and more interesting.

1. The concert hall was _____. (nice, fabulous)

2. It was _____ decorated in red and gold velvet. (handsomely, neatly)

3. The audience waited _____ for the concert to begin. (eagerly, happily)

4. The _____ conductor raised his baton. (talented, good)

5. The _____ orchestra came to attention. (big, huge)

6. The audience was _____ still. (very, absolutely)

7. The orchestra performed _____. (well, magnificently)

8. The tenor sang _____. (nicely, brilliantly)

9. The audience clapped _____. (enthusiastically, loudly)

10. It was a _____ concert. (splendid, good)

Underline the adjective or adverb in parentheses that makes each phrase clearer and more interesting.

11. a harp's (nice, delicate) tones

12. reacted (joyously, nicely)

13. a (difficult, hard) composition

14. (good, outstanding) performance

15. sang (well, beautifully)

16. played (remarkably, nicely)

17. a (world-famous, good) orchestra

18. performed (successfully, well)

Helping at Home

Say an adjective such as *green* or an adverb such as *creatively*. Can your child supply a matching noun such as *grass* or verb such as *draw*? Take turns giving each other modifiers. How quickly can you go? The first one to run out of ideas is out.

59

Varieties of Speech

A fifth grader might say "Hi! How are you?" when she greets a friend. Draw a line to another way to say this phrase to the person who might say it.

1. "Yo, man, what's happening?"   A. someone from the South

2. "Hello, my dear. How have you been?"   B. cool dude

3. "Hey, y'all, what y'all doing?"   C. grumpy old man

4. "Hi, how's it going?"   D. sweet old lady

5. "Umph. What's a matter with you?"   E. mother

Write the same sentence in three different ways to convey the emotions in parentheses.

6. (excitement)

_____

_____

7. (disappointment)

_____

_____

8. (surprise)

_____

_____

Have your child think of favorite characters from books, movies, and TV. How does their way of speaking show their age, personality, place of residence, etc.? Find photos of people in magazines or on the Internet. How might those characters speak?

Word Meanings

Match the words in the first column with the definitions in the second column. Each word will have more than one definition. Use a dictionary if needed.

1. palm _____

2. fiddle _____

3. court _____

4. vessel _____

5. mask _____

6. harp _____

7. prompt _____

8. sore _____

9. glare _____

10. cabinet _____

A. a tube in the body

B. a stringed instrument played with a bow

C. to dwell on a subject

D. angry

E. flat part of the hand

F. a face used for disguise

G. a harsh, bright light

H. to move hands and fingers restlessly

I. tender, painful

J. cupboard

K. on time

L. enclosed playing area

M. to assist an actor by saying his or her next words

N. type of tree

O. a stringed instrument played by plucking

P. a large boat

Q. to stare angrily

R. a place where judges hear cases

S. advisers to the president

T. to cover up; hide something

Helping at Home

Make sure your child has access to a print or online dictionary to use when doing homework. Model using a dictionary at your home when you read, watch news or documentary programs, or play word games.

Idioms, Proverbs, and Adages

Draw a line to match each idiom with its meaning.

1. Who let the cat out of the bag?

2. Can I add my two cents?

3. Don't cry over spilled milk.

4. Mark is a chip off the old block.

5. Nick is the apple of his mother's eye.

6. Julio can do that with one hand tied behind his back.

A. Don't worry about something that cannot be changed.

B. He can do it easily.

C. Can I give my opinion?

D. He is special.

E. He is like his father.

F. Who told the secret?

Draw a line to match the proverb or adage with its meaning.

7. A stitch in time saves nine.

8. Live and learn.

9. If at first you don't succeed, try, try again.

10. Slow and steady wins the race.

11. The early bird catches the worm.

12. Don't judge a book by its cover.

G. Keep working toward the goal.

H. Take time to fix something before it becomes a big problem.

I. Don't make a decision about something or someone by what you see on the outside.

J. Learn from your mistakes.

K. Don't give up because you make a mistake.

L. It is better to do things early than to put them off.

Helping at Home

Have your child research other common idiomatic expressions in English and choose a favorite. It could be *a penny for your thoughts* or *missed the boat*. Ask your child to illustrate the literal and figurative meanings of the expression.

Synonyms and Antonyms

Write the word that is the antonym of the other words. Use a dictionary if needed.

1. old   elderly   young   antique   aged   _____

2. chuckle   laugh   snicker   sigh   giggle   _____

3. screen   hide   conceal   cover   view   _____

4. mend   repair   fix   rip   patch   _____

5. cry   weep   laugh   sob   wail   _____

6. beautiful   stunning   hideous   gorgeous   _____

7. kind   pleasant   agreeable   unsociable   _____

8. tight   stretched   loose   taut   _____

Circle the synonym in parentheses for the bold word in each sentence.

9. We were **floating** down the river on our inner tubes. (gliding, sailing)

10. I was so **excited** about going to the beach that I could not sleep. (enthusiastic, nervous)

11. My brother **collects** autographs of movie stars. (gathers, finds)

12. Whitney has been **late** to class several times this year. (tardy, slow)

13. Jose needed a **plain** sheet of paper to draw his picture. (simple, ordinary)

14. Our class needs to inflate 50 balloons for the **celebration**. (party, parade)

15. Could I have a **piece** of your delicious apple pie? (section, slice)

16. Our class **constructed** a model of the solar system. (built, saw)

Helping at Home

"Catch" your child and other family members using overused or "dead" words such as *like, nice, said, very, cool,* or *fun.* Stop the person and challenge him or her to substitute a more interesting synonym. Let your child catch you using overused words, too.

Common Core State Standards for Math*

The following parent-friendly explanations of fifth grade Common Core math standards are provided to help you understand what your child will learn in school this year. Practice pages listed will help your child master each skill.

Complete Common Core State Standards may be found here: www.corestandards.org.

5.OA Operations and Algebraic Thinking

Write and interpret numerical expressions.
(Standards: 5.OA.A.1, 5.OA.A.2)

Your child will understand that when parentheses, brackets, and braces appear in math expressions, the operations inside (addition, subtraction, etc.) should be done first.
• **Practice pages: 68, 69**

Your child will write simple math expressions to state numerical calculations. For example, for "add 2 plus 3, then multiply by 5," your child will write $5 \times (2 + 3)$. • **Practice pages: 70, 71**

Analyze patterns and relationships.
(Standard: 5.OA.B.3)

Your child will pair the related numbers in a pattern and graph the numbers on a grid. For example, he or she might graph the number of miles that can be traveled on each gallon of gas. • **Practice pages: 72, 73**

5.NBT Number and Operations in Base Ten

Understand the place value system.
(Standards: 5.NBT.A.1, 5.NBT.A.2, 5.NBT.A.3a, 5.NBT.A.3b, 5.NBT.B.4)

Your child will work with multi-digit numbers and recognize that a digit in one place represents 10 times as much as it does in the place to its right and $\frac{1}{10}$ as much as it does in the place to its left. • **Practice page: 74**

Your child will work with zeros and powers of 10. He or she will understand that 10^2 means 10×10. Your child will multiply and divide decimals by powers of 10, moving the decimal point accordingly. • **Practice pages: 75, 76**

Your child will read and write decimals to the thousandths place. • **Practice page: 77**

Your child will compare two decimals to the thousandths place and tell which is greater or less.
• **Practice page: 78**

Your child will round decimals to any place. • **Practice page: 79**

Perform operations with multi-digit whole numbers and with decimals to hundredths.
(Standards: 5.NBT.B.5, 5.NBT.B.6, 5.NBT.B.7)

Your child will multiply large, multi-digit numbers. • **Practice pages: 80, 82**

Your child will divide numbers up to four digits by numbers up to two digits.
• **Practice pages: 81, 82**

Your child will add, subtract, multiply, and divide decimals to the hundredths place.
• **Practice pages: 83–88**

5.NF Number and Operations—Fractions

Use equivalent fractions as a strategy to add and subtract fractions.
(Standards: 5.NF.A.1, 5.NF.A.2)

Your child will add and subtract fractions with unlike denominators by rewriting them as equivalent fractions with like denominators. • **Practice pages: 89–93**

Your child will solve word problems that involve adding and subtracting fractions.
• **Practice pages: 94, 95, 105**

Apply and extend previous understandings of multiplication and division to multiply and divide fractions.
(Standards: 5.NF.B.3, 5.NF.B.4, 5.NF.B.6, 5.NF.B.7)

Your child will understand that a fraction such as $\frac{3}{4}$ is the same as "three divided by 4." He or she will solve word problems in which a whole number is divided into fractions.
• **Practice pages: 96, 97**

Your child will multiply whole numbers by fractions and multiply fractions by fractions. He or she will use visual models to understand what it means to multiply fractions.
• **Practice pages: 98–100**

Common Core State Standards for Math*

Your child will solve real-world problems and word problems that involve multiplying fractions.
• **Practice pages:** 101, 102, 105

Your child will solve mathematical problems and word problems that involve dividing whole numbers by fractions and dividing fractions by whole numbers. • **Practice pages:** 103–105

5.MD Measurement and Data

Convert like measurement units within a given measurement system.
(Standard: 5.MD.A.1)

Your child will convert measurements within the same measurement system. For example, he or she will convert feet to inches and miles to yards. He or she will use measurement conversions to solve real-world problems. • **Practice pages:** 106–108, 114

Represent and interpret data.
(Standard: 5.MD.B.2)

Your child will measure things in fractions of units (for example: $\frac{1}{4}$ inch, $\frac{1}{2}$ inch, etc.) and record the data using a line plot. He or she will use fractions to solve problems related to the data.
• **Practice page:** 109

Geometric measurement: understand concepts of volume and relate
volume to multiplication and to addition.
(Standards: 5.MD.C.3, 5.MD.C.4, 5.MD.C.5a, 5.MD.C.5b, 5.MD.C.5c)

Your child will understand that volume measures the capacity of three-dimensional figures. Volume is equal to the number of "unit cubes," or cubes with a side length of 1 unit, that can be packed without gaps into a solid figure. • **Practice pages:** 110, 111

Your child will calculate the volume of rectangular prisms (or box shapes) by multiplying length × width × height. • **Practice pages:** 112–114

Your child will calculate the volumes of individual parts of complex shapes and add them together to find the total volume. • **Practice page:** 115

5.G Geometry

Graph points on the coordinate plane to solve real-world and mathematical problems.
(Standards: 5.G.A.1, 5.G.A.2)

Your child will work with grids, or "coordinate planes," with numbered horizontal and vertical axes. He or she will use coordinates, or "ordered pairs" of numbers to pinpoint specific locations on the grid. • **Practice pages: 116, 117**

Your child will solve problems by graphing points on a coordinate plane. • **Practice page: 118**

Classify two-dimensional figures into categories based on their properties.
(Standards: 5.G.B.3, 5.G.B.4)

Your child will understand attributes of two-dimensional figures (examples: number of sides, number of corners, parallel or perpendicular lines) and use them to classify shapes.
• **Practice pages: 119–121**

Parentheses and Brackets in Expressions

Solve the problem within groupings first.
Example: $3 \times (5 + 4)$
$3 \times 9 = 27$

Evaluate each expression. Look for your answer swimming in the sea of answers.

1. $2 \times (4 - 2)$	2. $(3 + 13) - (2 + 8)$
3. $(452 - 448) \times 6$	4. $(18 - 3) \times 6$
5. $2 \times [5 \times (3 + 7)]$	6. $500 - [3 \times (20 + 80)]$

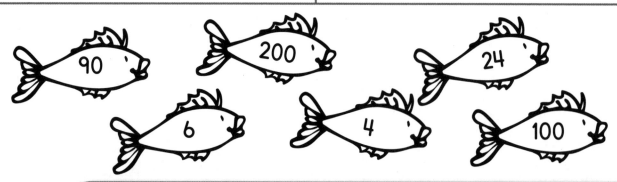

90   200   24   6   4   100

Helping at Home

Write a series of numbers, such as *68, 125, 4, 18, 100*, five times on a large sheet of paper. Can your child add operations symbols (+, −, ×, ÷), parentheses, and brackets to make five different expressions with five different values?

Parentheses and Brackets in Expressions

Evaluate each expression.

1. 3 + (8 – 1)	2. (16 – 7) × 5
3. 3 × [8 + (5 – 1)]	4. (7 + 3) + (12 – 7)
5. (3 + 5) × (4 + 8)	6. 11 + (13 – 8)
7. 3 + {20 – [3 × (2 + 4)]}	8. 6 + (3 + 12) – 2

Helping at Home

Choose a number such as *128*. Can you and your child each write an expression, including parentheses and brackets, that has that value? Compare the expressions you wrote. Let your child choose a number and play again.

Writing Expressions

Add 4 and 2 and then multiply by 5.

The order of operations says to multiply first.
But, the expression uses the word *then* to explain that the multiplication needs to happen *after* addition.

Use grouping symbols such as parentheses to write the expression.

(4 + 2) × 5 or 5 × (4 + 2)

Write each sentence as a numerical expression.

1. Add 5 and 6 and then multiply by 3.

2. Subtract 7 from 15 and then multiply by 4.

3. Add 6 and 10, subtract your answer from 20, and then multiply by 2.

4. Multiply the sums of 5 and 6 and 3 and 4.

5. Multiply the sum of 4 and 6 by 7.

6. Divide the sum of 5 and 9 by 2.

Challenge your child to look back to the expressions on page 68. Can he or she say and write words to describe each expression? For example, for item #1, the expression would be "subtract two from four and then multiply by 2."

Writing Expressions

Draw a line to match each expression with the phrase that describes it.

1. 3 times larger than the sum of 4 and 9

A. 20 – (3 + 4)

2. 20 less the sum of 3 and 4

B. (2 + 5) × (6 + 10)

3. the quotient of 15 and the sum of 2 and 3

C. (10 + 8) ÷ (10 – 7)

4. the product of the sums of 2 and 5 and 6 and 10

D. (12 – 7) × 3

5. 6 times larger than the difference of 10 and 7

E. (4 + 5) × 8

6. the quotient of the sum of 10 and 8 and the difference of 10 and 7

F. 6 × (10 – 7)

7. the sum of 4 and 5 multiplied by 8

G. 15 ÷ (2 + 3)

8. the difference of 12 and 7 multiplied by 3

H. 3 × (4 + 9)

Helping at Home
It may help your child to review the meanings of math-related words such as *sum, difference, product,* and *quotient.* Encourage your child to begin a list of math words and definitions. Make sure your child uses the terms correctly and comfortably.

Patterns and Relationships

Use the information to complete each section of the table.

A new country artist sold 1 million copies of his first album, 3 million copies of his second album, and 5 million copies of his third album. If the pattern continues, how many copies will he sell when he makes his fifth album?

1. Explain the pattern in words.	2.

2.

Album Number	Records Sold (in Millions)
1	
2	
3	
4	
5	

3. Use the table in question 2 to make a list of ordered pairs. The first pair has been done for you.

(1,1)

4. Graph your points on the coordinate plane below.

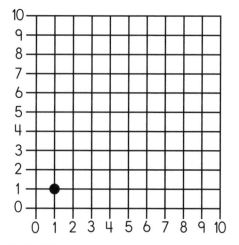

5. He will sell _____ copies of his fifth album.

Helping at Home

How old will your child be in 2020? 2035? 2050? Encourage your child to make a chart that shows his or her age in different years. Can your child use the data to create a set of ordered pairs and graph them on a coordinate plane?

Patterns and Relationships

Use the information to complete each section of the table.

Long-distance swimmers generally need to take more breaths as they near the end of a race. On lap 2, Mark took 2 breaths; he took 3 breaths on lap 4, and he took 4 breaths on lap 6. If the pattern continues, how many breaths will Mark take on lap 10?

1. Explain the pattern in words.	2.

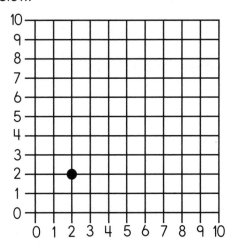

Lap Number	Breaths
2	
4	
6	
8	
10	

3. Use the table in question 2 to make a list of ordered pairs. The first pair has been done for you.

(2,2)

4. Graph your points on the coordinate plane below.

5. He will take _____ breaths on lap 10.

Helping at Home

Encourage your child to compare the four ways of showing information in boxes 1–4 on this page. Which way is easiest for your child to understand? Why? Spend some time working with your child on the method that he or she finds most difficult.

Place Value

How many tenths are in 34?

Use the nearest place values to find a more specific answer. Start at the decimal point. Look to the right to find tenths or hundredths. Look to the left to find ones, tens, or hundreds.

$$34.0 \leftarrow$$

There are 40 tenths in 34.

Answer each question. Some answers may be written as decimals.

1. How many tens are in 85?

2. How many tenths are in 5?

3. How many tens are in 235?

4. How many hundredths are in 0.5?

5. How many tens are in 153?

6. How many ones are in 512.5?

7. How many tenths are in 15.03?

8. Circle two numbers above. Explain how the 5s are different.

Helping at Home

Write a number such as *543210* on a large sheet of blank paper. Use a penny to represent a decimal point at different places in the number. For each position of the penny, can your child say the number? Can your child tell how many tens, tenths, etc.?

Multiplying Decimals by Powers of 10

To multiply by 10, move the decimal point **one** place to the right.

0.4

10 × 0.4 = 4

To multiply by 100, move the decimal point **two** places to the right.

0.40

100 × 0.4 = 40

To multiply by 1,000, move the decimal point **three** places to the right.

0.400

1,000 × 0.4 = 400

Find each product. Use mental math.

1. 10 × 0.06 =   100 × 0.06 =   1,000 × 0.06 =   10 × 0.6 =

2. 10 × 4.3 =   100 × 4.3 =   1,000 × 4.3 =   0.43 × 100 =

3. 0.653 × 1,000 =   1.09 × 10 =   21.3 × 10 =   10 × 0.007 =

4. 1,000 × 0.046 =   0.46 × 1,000 =   0.46 × 100 =   0.46 × 10 =

5. 1,000 × 3.9 =   0.0045 × 10 =   100 × 0.03 =   12.6 × 1,000 =

6. 1.234 × 100 =   0.11 × 1,000 =   0.11 × 10,000 =   0.11 × 100,000 =

Helping at Home

Encourage your child to think aloud while summarizing the rules at the top of this page. Ask, "When you multiply a decimal number, does it get larger or smaller? Does the decimal point move to the right or the left? Why?"

Multiplying Decimals by Powers of 10

Explain how many times you would move the decimal point and in which direction to solve each problem.

1. 5×10^2	2. 3×10^5
3. $50 \div 10^3$	4. $125 \div 10$
5. $840 \div 10^2$	6. 675×10^2
7. 10.034×10^4	8. $800.01 \div 10^4$

Helping at Home

Have your child choose several problems from this page to write out and solve by hand. For item #6, he or she would solve $675 \times 10 \times 10$. Does the solution match what your child arrived at through mental math? Which method is easier?

Reading and Writing Decimals

You should already know the place value names for numbers greater than 0. There are also names for place values after the decimal place.

thousands	hundreds	tens	ones		tenths	hundredths	thousandths
1	2	4	5	.	1	7	6

Study the following:

Decimal	Read As	Equivalent Fractions
0.1	one-tenth	$\frac{1}{10}$
0.7	seven-tenths	$\frac{7}{10}$
0.23	twenty-three hundredths	$\frac{23}{100}$
0.05	five-hundredths	$\frac{5}{100}$
0.783	seven hundred eighty-three thousandths	$\frac{783}{1000}$
0.045	forty-five thousandths	$\frac{45}{1000}$
2.6	two and six-tenths	$2\frac{6}{10}$
15.01	fifteen and one-hundredth	$15\frac{1}{100}$

Hint: Use "and" to separate a whole number from a fraction.

Fill in the blanks with the missing information.

1. 0.3   three-tenths   _____

2. 1.12   _____   _____

3. _____   two hundred twenty-one thousandths   _____

Helping at Home

Have your child visit Olympics.org and search for record times for the 100-meter dash or other events. Can your child say each finish time aloud? Can he or she write equivalent fractions for several of the top finish times?

Comparing Decimals

Comparing decimals is similar to comparing whole numbers.
1. Line up the numbers by place value.
2. Compare the digits from left to right.

Example 1 0.08 ◯ 0.8

1. Align: 0.08
              0.8

2. Compare. After the decimal point, you have a 0 and an 8. Because 8 is greater than 0, the greater number is 0.8.

0.08 **(<)** **0.8**

Example 2 11.13 ◯ 11.03

1. Align: 11.13
              11.03

2. Compare. The 11s before the decimal point are the same. After the decimal point, because 1 is greater than 0, the greater number is 1.

11.13 **(>)** **11.03**

Compare using <, >, or =.

1. 0.007 ◯ 0.07

2. 0.08 ◯ 0.8

3. 2.159 ◯ 2.259

4. 101.05 ◯ 101.005

5. 10.05 ◯ 10.005

6. 9.50 ◯ 7.05

7. 0.99 ◯ 0.009

8. 214.01 ◯ 214.001

9. 30.249 ◯ 30.429

10. 9.008 ◯ 9.08

11. 0.004 ◯ 4.00

12. 614.05 ◯ 614.05

13. 6.041 ◯ 6.401

14. 8.26 ◯ 8.026

15. 92.001 ◯ 92.001

16. 43.014 ◯ 43.104

© Carson-Dellosa • CD-704505

Helping at Home

To help your child complete problems on this page, encourage him or her to say each number aloud. Test your child's understanding by asking, "Which is greater—one tenth or one hundredth? One hundredth or one thousandth?"

Rounding Decimals

Round each number to the nearest tenth.

1. 0.57

2. 0.978

3. 1.56

4. 3.087

Round each number to the nearest hundredth.

5. 6.3465

6. 3.14579

7. 0.0081

8. 2.5869

Round each decimal to the nearest tenth and hundredth.

9. 3.0184

10. 29.962

Have fun working with the number Pi (3.1415926535…). Can your child round it to the nearest tenth? Hundredth? Thousandth? Ten-thousandth? Use the Internet to search for 100,000 digits of Pi. Can your child memorize the first ten digits?

Multiplying Multi-Digit Numbers

Step 1	Step 2	Step 3	Step 4
Multiply by the ones digit.	Multiply by the tens digit.	Multiply by the hundreds digit.	Add.

Step 1
Multiply by the ones digit.

$$\begin{array}{r} \overset{2}{8}72 \\ \times\ 494 \\ \hline 3,488 \end{array}$$

$4 \times 872 = 3,488$

Step 2
Multiply by the tens digit.

$$\begin{array}{r} \overset{6\ 1}{8}72 \\ \times\ 494 \\ \hline 3,488 \\ 78,48\underline{0} \end{array}$$

$90 \times 872 = 78,480$

Step 3
Multiply by the hundreds digit.

$$\begin{array}{r} \overset{2}{8}72 \\ \times\ 494 \\ \hline 3,488 \\ 78,48\underline{0} \\ 348,8\underline{00} \end{array}$$

$400 \times 872 = 348,800$

Step 4
Add.

$$\begin{array}{r} 872 \\ \times\ 494 \\ \hline 3,488 \\ 78,480 \\ +\ 348,800 \\ \hline 430,768 \end{array}$$

Multiply.

1. $\begin{array}{r} 762 \\ \times 381 \end{array}$

2. $\begin{array}{r} 503 \\ \times 741 \end{array}$

3. $\begin{array}{r} 638 \\ \times 897 \end{array}$

4. $\begin{array}{r} 982 \\ \times 872 \end{array}$

5. $\begin{array}{r} 594 \\ \times 439 \end{array}$

6. $\begin{array}{r} 287 \\ \times 287 \end{array}$

7. $\begin{array}{r} 758 \\ \times 439 \end{array}$

8. $\begin{array}{r} 165 \\ \times 825 \end{array}$

9. $\begin{array}{r} 284 \\ \times 833 \end{array}$

10. $\begin{array}{r} 477 \\ \times 360 \end{array}$

11. $\begin{array}{r} 383 \\ \times 103 \end{array}$

12. $\begin{array}{r} 460 \\ \times 342 \end{array}$

13. $\begin{array}{r} 598 \\ \times 636 \end{array}$

14. $\begin{array}{r} 963 \\ \times 328 \end{array}$

15. $\begin{array}{r} 789 \\ \times 951 \end{array}$

16. $\begin{array}{r} 4,610 \\ \times\ 239 \end{array}$

17. $\begin{array}{r} 3,944 \\ \times\ 307 \end{array}$

18. $\begin{array}{r} 2,775 \\ \times\ 173 \end{array}$

19. $\begin{array}{r} 1,615 \\ \times\ 239 \end{array}$

20. $\begin{array}{r} 2,138 \\ \times\ 256 \end{array}$

Helping at Home

Have your child research how many times, on average, people do things each day, such as yawn (12 times), blink (14,400 times), or burp (14 times). Ask your child to multiply the numbers by 365 to see how many times the events happen each year.

Dividing Multi-Digit Numbers

Divide **32)7,980**

Step 1
There are not enough thousands to divide. Estimate to place the first digit in the quotient.

Use rounding to estimate.

Think: 30)80
80 ÷ 30 is about 2

The first digit of the quotient will be in the hundreds place. - - - - - ⌐

Step 2
Multiply. Subtract. Compare. Bring down the next digit.

```
      2
32 ) 7,980      Multiply 2 × 32
    -64         Subtract 79 – 64
    158         Compare 15 < 32
                Bring down the 8.
```

Step 3
Multiply. Subtract. Compare. Bring down the next digit.

```
      249r12
32 ) 7,980
    -64
    158         Multiply 4 × 32
   -128         Subtract 158 – 128
    300         Compare 30 < 32
   -288         Bring down the 0.
     12         (Repeat steps.)
                The remainder must
                always be less than
                the divisor.
```

The digits are really coming down today!

Divide.

1. 46)857

2. 28)635

3. 32)8,329

4. 55)1,728

5. 21)4,670

6. 17)4,287

7. 58)2,439

8. 73)8,967

Helping at Home
Remind your child to line up numbers carefully in columns when doing long division problems. Suggest that he or she use a colored pencil to draw faint vertical lines between columns of numbers and to add zeros where needed.

Multiplying and Dividing Multi-Digit Numbers

Solve.

S   243 × 8 = _____

O   834 ÷ 8 = _____

E   9 × 6,418 = _____

Y   289 ÷ 72 = _____

K   53 × 28 = _____

A   2,566 ÷ 42 = _____

D   442 × 64 = _____

W   496 ÷ 74 = _____

J   221 × 628 = _____

U   2,720 ÷ 6 = _____

F   487 × 12 = _____

L   420 × 24 = _____

T   5,432 ÷ 55 = _____

N   989 × 62 = _____

C   4,277 ÷ 18 = _____

R   527 × 398 = _____

I   5,859 ÷ 55 = _____

H   3,789 ÷ 16 = _____

Each person below is answering the question, "How's business?" To decode their answers, solve the problems above. Find the answers in the codes below. Write the letter of each problem above the answer. Keep solving until you have decoded all three responses.

Soldier   "Mine is

| 138,788 | 453r2 | 1,944 | 98r42 |

| 5,844 | 106r29 | 61,318 | 57,762 |
,

| 98r42 | 61r4 | 61,318 | 1,484 | 1,944 |
"

Steak House Chef   "Mine is

| 6r52 | 104r2 | 209,746 | 1,944 | 57,762 |

| 28,288 | 106r29 | 1,944 | 236r13 |

| 4r1 | 57,762 | 61r4 | 209,746 |
"

Teacher   "Mine is

| 237r11 | 10,080 | 61r4 | 1,944 | 1,944 | 4r1 |
"

Brainstorm with your child real-life examples of times when people multiply and divide large numbers. Examples may include calculating how much food is needed for a large group or dividing a lottery jackpot by the number of winners.

Helping at Home

82

© Carson-Dellosa • CD-704505

Adding and Subtracting Decimals

Ginny took the money she earned babysitting and went to the movies. She spent **$3.90** for her ticket. Then, she spent **half** of the remaining money on popcorn. On the way home, she bought an ice cream cone for **$1.49**. When she got home, she had **$0.81** left of her earnings. How much did she earn babysitting?

$0.81	→	Start with the money left over.
+ 1.49	→	Add money spent on ice cream cone.
2.30	→	half of remaining money
+ 2.30	→	Add other half of money spent on popcorn.
4.60	→	money remaining after buying ticket
+ 3.90	→	Add money spent on ticket.
$8.50	→	**money that Ginny earned babysitting**

Solve each problem.

1. An owner of a retail clothing store bought a dress for $36.25 and sold it for $59.99. What was her profit?

2. A pair of running shoes costs $22.29. The store owner wanted to make a profit of $18.50. What should be the shoes' selling price?

3. Malcolm spent $48.74 on new speakers and $25.39 on computer games. After his purchases, he only had $0.58 left. How much money did Malcolm have before he went shopping?

4. In the town of Sleepy Oak, the fine for a speeding ticket is $32.65 + s dollars, where s is the miles per hour over the speed limit.

   A. What is the fine for going 38.4 miles per hour in a 25-miles-per-hour school zone?

   B. Mr. Taylor was fined $50.15 for speeding in the same school zone. How fast was he driving?

Helping at Home
Ask your child to spend an imaginary $1,000. What would he or she buy? Encourage your child to research prices of items including dollars and cents, make a list, and add. What if the amount were reduced to $700? What would your child subtract?

Multiplying Decimals

To multiply decimals, first multiply as you would with whole numbers. Then, count the total number of decimal places to the right of the decimal point in each factor. That is the number of decimal places in the product.

Examples:

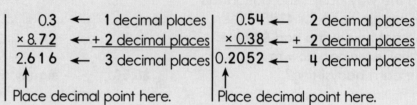

4.69 ← 2 decimal places	0.3 ← 1 decimal places	0.54 ← 2 decimal places
× 3 ← + 0 decimal places	× 8.72 ← + 2 decimal places	× 0.38 ← + 2 decimal places
14.07 ← 2 decimal places	2.616 ← 3 decimal places	0.2052 ← 4 decimal places
↑ Place decimal point here.	↑ Place decimal point here.	↑ Place decimal point here.

Place the decimal point in each answer.

1.
$$199.6 \times 8 = 15968$$
$$19.96 \times 8 = 15968$$
$$1.996 \times 8 = 15968$$
$$199.6 \times 0.8 = 15968$$
$$1.996 \times 0.8 = 15968$$

2.
$$300.4 \times 6 = 18024$$
$$30.04 \times 6 = 18024$$
$$3.004 \times 6 = 18024$$
$$300.4 \times 0.6 = 18024$$
$$3.004 \times 0.6 = 18024$$

3.
$$250.2 \times 5 = 12510$$
$$25.02 \times 5 = 12510$$
$$2.502 \times 5 = 12510$$
$$250.2 \times 0.5 = 12510$$
$$2.502 \times 0.5 = 12510$$

4.
$$15.84 \times 0.5 = 792$$
$$42.6 \times 0.6 = 2556$$
$$18.7 \times 0.7 = 1309$$
$$21.9 \times 0.4 = 876$$
$$19.4 \times 3.6 = 6984$$

5.
$$21.7 \times 4.2 = 9114$$
$$63.1 \times 2.2 = 13882$$
$$36.6 \times 4.7 = 17202$$
$$3.41 \times 6.2 = 21142$$
$$7.67 \times 1.3 = 9971$$

Helping at Home

For several problems on this page, ask your child to use a highlighter pen to highlight each place after the decimal in the factors. Then, he or she can count the number of places highlighted and write the decimal point in the product.

Multiplying Decimals

Find the missing digits in the following multiplication problems. Then, place the decimal point in the product.

1.
```
    1̲88
  × 1̲2
   379
 +1880
  2256
```

2.
```
    □.1 9
  × 0.3□
   1038
 +15570
  16608
```

3.
```
   8.□6
  × □.3
   2628
 +35040
  37668
```

4.
```
    □5.6
  × □.1
    256
  +7680
   7936
```

5.
```
   4.□□
  × 2.□
    432
  +8640
   9072
```

6.
```
    □4.9
  × □.7
   1043
  +2980
   4023
```

7.
```
   □5.□
  × □.5
    755
  +6040
   6795
```

8.
```
    □.1 2
  × 0.□□
    312
  +18720
   19032
```

Helping at Home

Ask your child if it is necessary to fill in the digits in the factors in each problem on this page before placing the decimal point in the product. Can your child explain why not? Look back to the rules explained on page 84 for help.

Dividing Decimals

Divide **2.5 ÷ 4**

Step 1
Divide the tenths.

```
   0.6
4 ) 2.5
  - 2 4
      1
```

Step 2
Write a **0** in the hundredths place.

```
    0.62
4 ) 2.50      ← Write a 0 here.
  - 2 4
     10       ← Write a 0 here.
    - 8         Divide by 4.
      2
```

Step 3
Write a **0** in the thousandths place. Bring down and divide.

```
    0.625
4 ) 2.500
  - 2 4
     10
    - 8
     20
   - 20
      0
```

Divide. Use multiplication to check your work.

1. $5\overline{)2.7}$ 2. $4\overline{)4.6}$ 3. $6\overline{)5.7}$ 4. $4\overline{)7.3}$ 5. $8\overline{)2.5}$

6. $4\overline{)0.31}$ 7. $5\overline{)8.1}$ 8. $4\overline{)6.3}$ 9. $5\overline{)0.73}$ 10. $4\overline{)4.2}$

11. $5\overline{)4.19}$ 12. $5\overline{)3.74}$ 13. $4\overline{)53.4}$ 14. $2\overline{)0.13}$ 15. $5\overline{)75.02}$

Helping at Home
Ask your child to imagine that a pizza costs $9.99. How much would each person's share cost if two people split the pizza? Four people? Five people?

Dividing Decimals

To divide by a decimal number, you must move the decimal to make the divisor a whole number. To make the divisor a whole number, multiply both the divisor and dividend by 10, 100, or 1,000.

Example: $0.08\overline{)6.081}$ = $8\overline{)608.1}$

Divide **5.44 ÷ 1.6**

Step 1
Move the decimal point one place to the right to make the divisor a whole number.

$1.6\overline{)5.44}$ ⟵ Multiply by 10.

Step 2
Place the decimal point in the quotient. Divide as you would with whole numbers.

$$
\begin{array}{r}
3.4 \\
16\overline{)54.4} \\
-48 \\
\hline
64 \\
-64 \\
\hline
0
\end{array}
$$

Divide. Use multiplication to check your work.

1. $0.6\overline{)5.4}$

2. $0.9\overline{)0.18}$

3. $1.4\overline{)13.86}$

4. $0.8\overline{)0.68}$

5. $1.7\overline{)10.54}$

6. $2.4\overline{)16.8}$

7. $0.07\overline{)0.35}$

8. $0.02\overline{)0.76}$

9. $0.05\overline{)0.15}$

10. $3.2\overline{)13.76}$

11. $0.03\overline{)0.45}$

12. $0.8\overline{)0.25}$

Helping at Home
For each item on this page, ask your child to tell if the divisor was multiplied by 10, 100, or 1000 to make a whole number.

Word Problems with Decimals

Sound energy can be measured in watts. This table shows the energy output of some musical instruments.

How many snare drums would it take to produce 73.8 watts of energy?

Think: 73.8 ÷ 12.3

$$
\begin{array}{r}
6 \\
123 \overline{\smash{)}738} \\
-738 \\
\hline
0
\end{array}
$$

So, **6** snare drums can produce 73.8 watts of energy.

Instrument	Energy Output
Piano	0.44 watts
Trombone	6.4 watts
Snare Drum	12.3 watts
Human Voice	0.000024 watts

Use the table to solve the problems.

1. How many trombones would it take to produce 1,280 watts of energy?

2. A piano can produce 8 times as much sound energy as a flute. How much energy does a flute produce?

3. About how many pianos playing together will produce the same sound energy as 1 snare drum?

4. A snare drum, a piano, and a trombone are all playing at once.
   A. What is the combined energy output of the instruments?

   B. What is the average energy output of the instruments?

5. How many pianos would produce 4.84 watts of energy?

Helping at Home

Ask your child to use the table at the top of this page to write another word problem for you to solve. It should include words such as *combined* or *for each* that tell which operation must be used to solve the problem. Write a word problem for your child to solve, too.

Lowest Common Denominator

To find the **lowest common denominator** (LCD):
1. List the multiples of each denominator.
2. The LCD is the least common multiple.

$$\frac{1}{4} = \frac{}{8} \longleftarrow \text{The LCD of 4 and 8}$$

$$\frac{1}{4} = \frac{1 \times 2}{4 \times 2} = \frac{2}{8}$$

$$\frac{1}{4} = \frac{2}{8}$$

Find the LCD of $\frac{1}{4}$ and $\frac{3}{8}$. Rewrite each fraction using the LCD.

1. List the multiples of each denominator.

$$4 = 4, \circledast{8}, 12, 16, 20, 24,\ldots$$

$$8 = \circledast{8}, 16, 24,\ldots$$

2. The LCD = 8.

$$\frac{3}{8} = \frac{}{8} \longleftarrow \text{The LCD of 4 and 8}$$

$$\frac{3}{8} = \frac{3 \times 1}{8 \times 1} = \frac{3}{8}$$

$$\frac{3}{8} = \frac{3}{8}$$

Find the lowest common denominator of each pair of fractions. Then, rewrite each fraction using the new common denominator.

1. $\frac{2}{3}, \frac{5}{6}$

2. $\frac{1}{2}, \frac{1}{4}$

3. $\frac{2}{5}, \frac{1}{10}$

4. $\frac{3}{4}, \frac{1}{12}$

5. $\frac{1}{7}, \frac{2}{14}$

6. $\frac{6}{9}, \frac{1}{3}$

7. $\frac{1}{10}, \frac{3}{5}$

8. $\frac{2}{3}, \frac{1}{2}$

9. $\frac{3}{4}, \frac{3}{5}$

Helping at Home
Write these fractions on index cards: $\frac{1}{2}, \frac{2}{3}, \frac{2}{4}, \frac{4}{5}, \frac{2}{6}, \frac{5}{7}, \frac{3}{8}, \frac{5}{9},$ and $\frac{7}{10}$. Have your child draw two cards and determine the lowest common denominator for the pair of fractions. Can he or she write two equivalent fractions using the LCD?

Adding Fractions with Unlike Denominators

To add fractions with unlike denominators:

$$2\frac{1}{3} \rightarrow \frac{1 \times 4}{3 \times 4} \rightarrow \frac{4}{12}$$
$$+ 3\frac{3}{4} \rightarrow \frac{3 \times 3}{4 \times 3} \rightarrow \frac{9}{12}$$
$$5 \qquad\qquad \frac{13}{12}$$
$$= 5 + 1\frac{1}{12} = 6\frac{1}{12}$$

1. Find the lowest common denominator (LCD).
2. Rewrite each fraction using the LCD.
3. Add.
4. Simplify if possible.

$$1\frac{7}{8} \xrightarrow{} \frac{7}{8}$$
$$+ 2\frac{1}{4} \rightarrow \frac{1 \times 2}{4 \times 2} \rightarrow \frac{2}{8}$$
$$3 \qquad\qquad \frac{9}{8}$$
$$= 3 + 1\frac{1}{8} = 4\frac{1}{8}$$

Add. Simplify if possible.

1. $1\frac{3}{8}$
$+ 4\frac{1}{6}$

2. $2\frac{3}{4}$
$+ 3\frac{1}{5}$

3. $5\frac{1}{3}$
$+ 1\frac{5}{6}$

4. $3\frac{2}{3}$
$+ 2\frac{1}{4}$

5. $6\frac{1}{2}$
$+ \quad\frac{3}{4}$

6. $5\frac{2}{5}$
$+ 2\frac{1}{3}$

7. $4\frac{1}{6}$
$+ 2\frac{3}{4}$

8. $1\frac{7}{8}$
$+ 2\frac{1}{6}$

9. $4\frac{5}{12}$
$+ 2\frac{5}{6}$

10. $1\frac{2}{5}$
$+ 3\frac{7}{10}$

11. $2\frac{3}{8}$
$+ 7\frac{1}{2}$

12. $6\frac{7}{11}$
$+ 5\frac{1}{2}$

Subtracting Fractions with Unlike Denominators

To subtract fractions with unlike denominators:

$$\frac{2}{5} \longrightarrow \frac{2 \times 3}{5 \times 3} \longrightarrow \frac{6}{15}$$
$$-\frac{1}{3} \longrightarrow \frac{1 \times 5}{3 \times 5} \longrightarrow \frac{5}{15}$$
$$\frac{1}{15}$$

1. Find the lowest common denominator (LCD).
2. Rewrite each fraction using the LCD.
3. Subtract.
4. Simplify if possible.

$$\frac{5}{8} \longrightarrow \frac{5 \times 3}{8 \times 3} \longrightarrow \frac{15}{24}$$
$$-\frac{1}{3} \longrightarrow \frac{1 \times 3}{3 \times 8} \longrightarrow \frac{8}{24}$$
$$\frac{7}{24}$$

Subtract. Simplify if possible.

1. $\frac{2}{3}$
   $-\frac{1}{4}$

2. $\frac{4}{5}$
   $-\frac{1}{2}$

3. $\frac{1}{2}$
   $-\frac{1}{3}$

4. $\frac{5}{7}$
   $-\frac{1}{2}$

5. $\frac{1}{2}$
   $-\frac{2}{9}$

6. $\frac{2}{3}$
   $-\frac{2}{7}$

7. $\frac{3}{4}$
   $-\frac{1}{5}$

8. $\frac{4}{5}$
   $-\frac{2}{7}$

9. $\frac{3}{5}$
   $-\frac{2}{9}$

10. $\frac{7}{8}$
    $-\frac{2}{5}$

11. $\frac{5}{6}$
    $-\frac{1}{7}$

12. $\frac{9}{11}$
    $-\frac{1}{6}$

Helping at Home

Challenge your child to make a flow chart that gives step-by-step directions for adding fractions with like denominators, adding fractions with unlike denominators, subtracting fractions with like denominators, and subtracting fractions with unlike denominators.

Subtracting Fractions from a Whole Number

To subtract a fraction from a whole number:

$$3 \longrightarrow 2\frac{4}{4}$$
$$-\frac{1}{4} \longrightarrow -\frac{1}{4}$$
$$\overline{2\frac{3}{4}}$$

1. Rewrite the whole number as an equivalent fraction using the lowest common denominator (LCD).
2. Subtract.

$$2 \longrightarrow 1\frac{6}{6}$$
$$-\frac{5}{6} \longrightarrow -\frac{5}{6}$$
$$\overline{1\frac{1}{6}}$$

Subtract.

1. $\begin{array}{r} 5 \\ -\frac{7}{8} \\ \hline \end{array}$

2. $\begin{array}{r} 3 \\ -\frac{1}{3} \\ \hline \end{array}$

3. $\begin{array}{r} 6 \\ -\frac{7}{9} \\ \hline \end{array}$

4. $\begin{array}{r} 4 \\ -\frac{2}{5} \\ \hline \end{array}$

5. $\begin{array}{r} 8 \\ -\frac{4}{5} \\ \hline \end{array}$

6. $\begin{array}{r} 5 \\ -\frac{4}{9} \\ \hline \end{array}$

7. $\begin{array}{r} 12 \\ -\frac{3}{11} \\ \hline \end{array}$

8. $\begin{array}{r} 9 \\ -\frac{8}{9} \\ \hline \end{array}$

9. $\begin{array}{r} 7 \\ -\frac{1}{3} \\ \hline \end{array}$

10. $\begin{array}{r} 10 \\ -\frac{1}{5} \\ \hline \end{array}$

11. $\begin{array}{r} 12 \\ -\frac{7}{10} \\ \hline \end{array}$

12. $\begin{array}{r} 8 \\ -\frac{5}{6} \\ \hline \end{array}$

Helping at Home

Give a mixed number that equals a whole number, such as $2\frac{5}{5}$ or $8\frac{3}{3}$. Can your child provide the equivalent whole number? Have your child give you mixed numbers, too, and see how fast you can go. The first one to miss an answer is out.

Subtracting Mixed Numbers

To subtract mixed numbers:
1. Find the lowest common denominator (LCD).
2. Rewrite the fraction(s) using the LCD.
3. Rewrite again, if needed, to subtract.
4. Subtract.
5. Simplify if possible.

Steps 1 & 2

$$8\frac{1}{3} \longrightarrow 8\frac{8}{24} \longrightarrow 7\frac{32}{24}$$
$$-6\frac{5}{8} \longrightarrow 6\frac{15}{24} \longrightarrow 6\frac{15}{24}$$
$$\overline{\phantom{-6\frac{5}{8}}\quad 1\frac{17}{24}}$$

Step 3

$$8\frac{8}{24} = 7 + 1 + \frac{8}{24}$$
$$= 7 + \frac{24}{24} + \frac{8}{24}$$
$$= 7 + \frac{32}{24}$$

Subtract. Simplify if possible.

1. $\quad 4\frac{1}{3}$
    $-\ 2\frac{1}{2}$

2. $\quad 6\frac{1}{8}$
    $-\ 5\frac{1}{6}$

3. $\quad 5\frac{1}{4}$
    $-\ 3\frac{1}{2}$

4. $\quad 8\frac{3}{5}$
    $-\ 5\frac{1}{3}$

5. $\quad 6\frac{3}{8}$
    $-\ 5\frac{3}{4}$

6. $\quad 4\frac{2}{9}$
    $-\ 3\frac{2}{3}$

7. $\quad 9\frac{1}{6}$
    $-\ 7\frac{1}{3}$

8. $\quad 5\frac{2}{5}$
    $-\ 3\frac{7}{10}$

9. $\quad 6\frac{1}{3}$
    $-\ 4\frac{5}{8}$

10. $\quad 7\frac{1}{4}$
    $-\ 3\frac{7}{8}$

11. $\quad 9\frac{3}{10}$
    $-\ 5\frac{4}{5}$

12. $\quad 3\frac{5}{12}$
    $-\ 2\frac{2}{3}$

© Carson-Dellosa • CD-704505

Helping at Home

Ask your child to choose one problem he or she solved on this page. Challenge your child to explain how he or she used multiplication (to write equivalent fractions), division (to simplify the solution), and subtraction to find the answer.

Word Problems with Fractions

Read the scenario. Then, answer each question. Check the answer for reasonableness.

Four classmates, Rachel, Greg, Ethan, and Sarah, are competing in an obstacle course. The course is 1 mile long. Each person must complete one part of the competition. The course begins with running through tires for $\frac{1}{6}$ mile, dribbling a basketball for $\frac{1}{4}$ mile, running $\frac{1}{2}$ mile, and then crossing the monkey bars.

1. If Rachel runs through the tires for $\frac{1}{6}$ of a mile and Greg dribbles the basketball for $\frac{1}{4}$ mile, what fraction of the course have Rachel and Greg completed?

2. A. If Ethan then runs for $\frac{1}{2}$ mile, how much of the course have Rachel, Greg, and Ethan completed?

   B. What fraction of the 1-mile course must Sarah cross on the monkey bars?

3. A. What fraction of the course did the boys, Greg and Ethan, cover?

   B. What fraction did the girls, Rachel and Sarah, cover?

4. The team took 25 minutes to complete the race. If Rachel took $5\frac{1}{4}$ minutes, Greg took $7\frac{1}{4}$ minutes, and Sarah took $6\frac{1}{6}$ minutes, how long did it take Ethan to run the $\frac{1}{2}$ mile?

Ask your child to use the illustration at the top of this page to write another word problem for you to solve. Write a problem for your child to solve, too.

Word Problems with Fractions

Use the table to solve each problem. Write the answer in simplest form. Check the answer for reasonableness.

Jobs	Tasha's Time per Job	Tyrone's Time per Job
Homework	$2\frac{1}{4}$ hours	$1\frac{2}{3}$ hours
Clean bathroom	$\frac{3}{4}$ hour	$\frac{1}{2}$ hour
Clean bedroom	$\frac{1}{3}$ hour	1 hour
Walk dog	$\frac{1}{2}$ hour	$\frac{3}{4}$ hour

1. How much total time does it take both Tasha and Tyrone to do their homework?

2. How much more time does Tasha spend on her homework than Tyrone?

3. How much more time does Tyrone spend cleaning his bedroom than Tasha?

4. If Tyrone comes home from school, does his homework, and then walks the dog, how much time will it take him?

5. If Tasha cleans once a week, how much time does she spend cleaning the bathroom and bedroom per week?

6. If Tyrone cleans the bathroom two times a week and Tasha cleans the bathroom only once a week, who spends more time cleaning the bathroom?

Helping at Home

Talk about what it means to check your answers for reasonableness. Ask your child to explain why an answer of $8\frac{1}{2}$ hours would not be reasonable for item #1 on this page. Talk about why $\frac{1}{4}$ hour would not be a reasonable answer for item #5.

Changing Improper Fractions

$\frac{14}{3}$ can be rewritten as $14 \div 3$ or $3\overline{)14}$.

$\frac{14}{3}$ is an improper fraction.

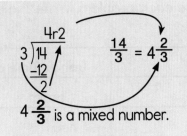

$\frac{14}{3} = 4\frac{2}{3}$

$4\frac{2}{3}$ is a mixed number.

The numerator becomes 2; the denominator stays 3.

Use division to change each improper fraction into a whole number.

1. $\frac{15}{2}$

2. $\frac{7}{4}$

3. $\frac{20}{7}$

4. $\frac{43}{5}$

5. $\frac{23}{8}$

6. $\frac{21}{5}$

7. $\frac{31}{12}$

8. $\frac{5}{2}$

9. $\frac{13}{8}$

10. $\frac{11}{4}$

11. $\frac{49}{9}$

12. $\frac{41}{6}$

13. $\frac{23}{3}$

14. $\frac{45}{4}$

15. $\frac{60}{5}$

Helping at Home

Help your child complete this page by asking, "How many times does the denominator go into the numerator?" For item #1, ask, "How many times does 2 go into 15? How many are left over? How does this help you write the answer $7\frac{1}{2}$?"

Partitioning Whole Numbers

Solve each problem. Leave your answer as a fraction or mixed number in simplified form.

1. Cindy baked 2 apple pies for herself and 7 other friends. If she divides the pies evenly among the 8 people, what fraction of pie will each person get?

2. Chang has 16 cups of cake batter, and he plans to divide it evenly to make 24 cupcakes. How many cups of batter will be in each cupcake?

3. Dominique needs 6 cups of dog food to feed her 4 dogs. If each dog gets the same amount of food, how many cups of food does each dog eat?

4. Gabe needs to cut an 8-foot piece of plywood into 16 equivalent pieces for a fence. How wide will each piece be if all are the same length?

5. A baker purchases flour in 25-pound bags and then separates it equally into 4 containers for storage. How many pounds of flour are in each container?

6. Dylan uses 4 cups of shredded cheese on 3 pizzas. How many cups of cheese are on each pizza?

Give everyday examples of things that are divided or shared, such as three gallons of ice cream for 20 kids, four toys for five puppies, or 10 sleds for 12 riders. Have your child give you the fraction that represents each situation ($\frac{3}{20}$, $\frac{4}{5}$, $\frac{10}{12}$).

Multiplying Fractions

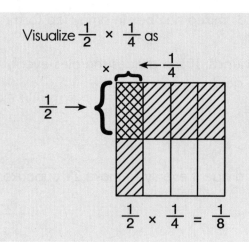

Visualize $\frac{1}{2} \times \frac{1}{4}$ as

$$\frac{1}{2} \times \frac{1}{4} = \frac{1}{8}$$

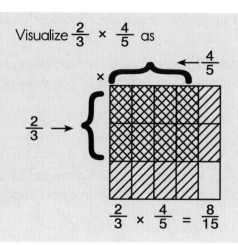

Visualize $\frac{2}{3} \times \frac{4}{5}$ as

$$\frac{2}{3} \times \frac{4}{5} = \frac{8}{15}$$

Multiply using the visual fraction model.

1.

$$\frac{1}{3} \times \frac{2}{5} = \underline{\quad}$$

2.

$$\frac{1}{4} \times \frac{1}{3} = \underline{\quad}$$

3.

$$\frac{1}{2} \times \frac{1}{2} = \underline{\quad}$$

4.

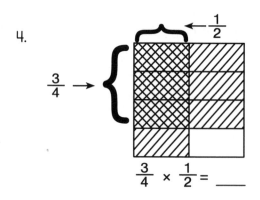

$$\frac{3}{4} \times \frac{1}{2} = \underline{\quad}$$

Helping at Home

Have your child draw a 3 × 4 grid of 12 boxes. How many different fractions can be shown with the model? Can your child shade different numbers of columns and rows to show these multiplication problems: $\frac{1}{4} \times \frac{1}{3}$, $\frac{1}{2} \times \frac{2}{3}$, $\frac{1}{4} \times \frac{2}{3}$?

Multiplying Fractions

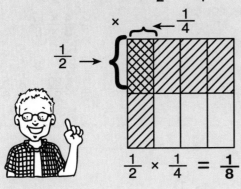

When multiplying $\frac{1}{2} \times \frac{1}{4}$:

$\frac{1}{2} \times \frac{1}{4} = \frac{1}{8}$

Multiply the numerators.
Multiply the denominators.

$$\frac{1}{2} \times \frac{1}{4} = \frac{1 \times 1}{2 \times 4} = \frac{1}{8}$$

$$\frac{3}{4} \times \frac{1}{7} = \frac{1 \times 3}{4 \times 7} = \frac{3}{28}$$

Multiply. Simplify if possible.

1. $\frac{1}{2} \times \frac{3}{4} =$ 2. $\frac{2}{3} \times \frac{1}{5} =$ 3. $\frac{2}{5} \times \frac{1}{3} =$ 4. $\frac{5}{6} \times \frac{1}{2} =$

5. $\frac{1}{4} \times \frac{3}{8} =$ 6. $\frac{5}{12} \times \frac{1}{2} =$ 7. $\frac{1}{2} \times \frac{5}{7} =$ 8. $\frac{1}{3} \times \frac{1}{4} =$

9. $\frac{1}{5} \times \frac{2}{5} =$ 10. $\frac{3}{5} \times \frac{1}{2} =$ 11. $\frac{3}{4} \times \frac{3}{5} =$ 12. $\frac{3}{4} \times \frac{1}{8} =$

13. $\frac{2}{5} \times \frac{3}{5} =$ 14. $\frac{1}{2} \times \frac{1}{2} =$ 15. $\frac{2}{3} \times \frac{2}{3} =$ 16. $\frac{3}{8} \times \frac{1}{2} =$

17. $\frac{5}{7} \times \frac{1}{3} =$ 18. $\frac{1}{2} \times \frac{3}{7} =$ 19. $\frac{5}{8} \times \frac{1}{3} =$ 20. $\frac{5}{6} \times \frac{1}{3} =$

Helping at Home

Look closely at the model at the top of the page with your child. Explain that multiplying $\frac{1}{2} \times \frac{1}{4}$ is the same as asking, "What is $\frac{1}{2}$ of $\frac{1}{4}$?" Help your child think of a real-world example such as, "What is $\frac{1}{4}$ of $\frac{1}{2}$ of a stack of trading cards?"

Multiplying Mixed Numbers

$2\frac{1}{4} \times 1\frac{1}{2} = \frac{9 \times 3}{4 \times 2}$

$= \frac{9 \times 3}{4 \times 2}$

$= \frac{27}{8}$

$= 3\frac{3}{8}$

When multiplying mixed numbers:
1. Rewrite the numbers as improper fractions.
2. Multiply the numerators.
3. Multiply the denominators.
4. Simplify if possible.

$1\frac{1}{3} \times 2\frac{1}{8} = \frac{4 \times 17}{3 \times 8}$

$= \frac{4 \times 17}{3 \times 8}$

$= \frac{68}{24}$

$= 2\frac{20}{24} = 2\frac{5}{6}$

Multiply. Simplify if possible.

1. $3\frac{3}{4} \times 2\frac{2}{3} =$

2. $1\frac{1}{4} \times 2\frac{1}{2} =$

3. $2\frac{1}{5} \times 2\frac{1}{4} =$

4. $1\frac{1}{5} \times 2\frac{1}{6} =$

5. $1\frac{3}{5} \times 1\frac{2}{5} =$

6. $2\frac{1}{2} \times 3\frac{1}{3} =$

7. $4\frac{1}{2} \times 1\frac{2}{3} =$

8. $2\frac{4}{5} \times 5\frac{1}{4} =$

9. $2\frac{3}{8} \times 2\frac{1}{3} =$

10. $1\frac{4}{5} \times 1\frac{1}{4} =$

11. $1\frac{3}{7} \times 1\frac{3}{8} =$

12. $1\frac{1}{2} \times 3\frac{2}{3} =$

13. $4\frac{1}{2} \times 1\frac{2}{5} =$

14. $2\frac{2}{3} \times 3\frac{1}{2} =$

Helping at Home

Demonstrate a trick for changing mixed numbers to improper fractions. Multiply the denominator by the whole number (for the first fraction in item #1, multiply $4 \times 3 = 12$). Then, add the numerator and write the sum over the denominator ($12 + 3 = 15 = \frac{15}{4}$).

Word Problems with Fractions

Solve each problem. Write the answer in simplified form.

1. Cody is making dinner for a group of his friends. He is making a recipe for stuffed chilies that uses $1\frac{3}{4}$ cups of cream cheese. Cody will only need to make $\frac{2}{3}$ of the recipe. How much cream cheese should he use?

2. A 2-serving recipe for chicken mole calls for $\frac{3}{12}$ teaspoons of chili powder and $1\frac{1}{2}$ tablespoons of olive oil. How much of each ingredient is needed to make 3 servings?

3. Cody has $\frac{7}{8}$ pound of cheese. He uses $\frac{1}{7}$ of this in his quesadillas. Since there are 16 ounces in 1 pound, how many ounces of cheese does Cody use in his quesadillas?

Solve problems 4–6 using this recipe.

Chilaquillas (Serves 6)	
1 dozen tortillas	$\frac{2}{3}$ cup chopped green onions
$2\frac{1}{2}$ cups grated jack cheese	$2\frac{1}{4}$ teaspoons chili powder
$1\frac{1}{3}$ cups tomato sauce	$\frac{1}{2}$ teaspoon crushed oregano
$1\frac{1}{4}$ cups low fat cottage cheese	$\frac{1}{4}$ cup oil

4. Cody will need enough chilaquillas to serve 8 people. By what number should the recipe be multiplied to make enough for all 8 people?

5. How much tomato sauce is required if the recipe is multiplied by $1\frac{1}{3}$?

6. How many cups of chopped green onions will be needed if the recipe is tripled?

7. Cody's recipe instructs him to bake at 205°C. He can convert this temperature to degrees Fahrenheit (°F) using this formula:

$$°F = \frac{9}{5} \times °C + 32$$

What cooking temperature should he use in degrees Fahrenheit?

Helping at Home
Invite your child to find a recipe to prepare for your family. Challenge him or her to multiply the ingredients to make the right number of servings for your family members. For each ingredient, what fraction of the package will be used?

Word Problems with Fractions

During Year 2, the size of a pond decreases to $\frac{1}{3}$ of what it was in Year 1. Assume that the same decrease occurs during Year 3. What fraction of the pond will remain after Year 3?

Picture It
Here is a model of the information.

Year 1

Year 2

Year 3

Solve It
Use the model to help you solve the problem.
Let 1 represent the whole pond in Year 1.

After Year 2, the pond is $\frac{1}{3}$ the size of Year 1.
Find the fraction of the pond remaining after Year 2.
$\frac{1}{3} \times 1 = \frac{1}{3}$

After Year 3, the pond is $\frac{1}{3}$ the size of Year 2.
Find the fraction of the pond remaining after Year 3.
$\frac{1}{3} \times \frac{1}{3} = \frac{1}{9}$

After Year 3, the pond will be $\frac{1}{9}$ the size it was in Year 1.

Solve each problem. Draw a model to help you.

1. Suppose every bounce of a ball is $\frac{2}{3}$ the height of its previous bounce. What fraction of the original height will the height of Bounce 3 be?

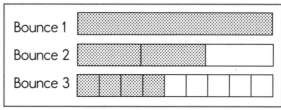

On Bounce 3, the ball will bounce to _____ of its original height.

2. Suppose a ball is dropped from its original height of 2 meters. Every bounce of the ball is $\frac{1}{2}$ the height of its previous bounce. How high will the ball bounce on Bounce 3?
   On Bounce 3, the ball will bounce _____ meter high.

3. A different ball is dropped from a height of 10 meters. On each bounce, it reaches $\frac{4}{5}$ of the height of its previous bounce. How high will the ball bounce on its third bounce?
   The ball will bounce _____ meters high on its third bounce.

© Carson-Dellosa • CD-704505

Helping at Home

Challenge your child to create a visual model showing what fraction of students in his or her class might be present or absent for each day of a five-day week. Ask your child to write a word problem for you to solve based on the model.

Dividing Fractions and Whole Numbers

When dividing fractions and whole numbers, first rename the whole number as a fraction with a denominator of 1.

To divide a fraction by a whole number:

Divide $\frac{4}{5} \div 8$

$\frac{4}{5} \div 8 = \frac{4}{5} \div \frac{8}{1}$ 　　Write the whole number as a fraction with a denominator of 1.

$\quad\quad = \frac{4}{5} \times \frac{1}{8}$ 　　Multiply $\frac{4}{5}$ by the reciprocal of $\frac{8}{1}$.

$\quad\quad = \frac{4 \times 1}{5 \times 8}$

$\quad\quad = \frac{4}{40}$

$\quad\quad = \frac{1}{10}$ 　　Reduce the answer to the lowest terms.

To divide a whole number by a fraction:

Divide $5 \div \frac{3}{4}$

$5 \div \frac{3}{4} = \frac{5}{1} \div \frac{3}{4}$ 　　Write the whole number as a fraction with a denominator of 1.

$\quad\quad = \frac{5}{1} \times \frac{4}{3}$ 　　Multiply $\frac{5}{1}$ by the reciprocal of $\frac{3}{4}$.

$\quad\quad = \frac{5 \times 4}{1 \times 3}$

$\quad\quad = \frac{20}{3}$

$\quad\quad = 6\frac{2}{3}$ 　　Change improper fractions to mixed numbers.

Divide. Write each quotient in its simplest form.

1. $6 \div \frac{4}{9} =$

2. $5 \div \frac{1}{7} =$

3. $\frac{4}{7} \div 8 =$

4. $\frac{6}{5} \div 2 =$

5. $\frac{3}{5} \div 4 =$

6. $\frac{5}{8} \div 5 =$

7. $\frac{9}{10} \div 4 =$

8. $\frac{1}{6} \div 3 =$

9. $\frac{9}{4} \div 6 =$

10. $\frac{5}{3} \div 4 =$

11. $\frac{4}{3} \div 5 =$

12. $\frac{8}{5} \div 5 =$

Helping at Home

Write numbers 1–9 and symbols ÷ and × on small slips of paper. In the center of a large sheet of paper, draw two horizontal lines. Ask your child to move the numbers and symbols above, below, and between the lines to act out solving the problems on this page.

Word Problems with Fractions

Draw a line to match each scenario to the correct division problem. Then, solve.

1. How many pieces of rope will you have if you cut a 2-foot piece of rope into $\frac{1}{4}$ -foot sections?

   A. $3\frac{1}{2} \div 7$

2. Jennifer has $3\frac{1}{2}$ cups of jelly beans to share with 7 friends. How many cups does each person get?

   B. $7 \div 3\frac{1}{2}$

3. Nadia made 4 cups of tea. She wants to pour it into glasses that each hold $\frac{1}{2}$ cup. How many glasses will she fill?

   C. $2 \div \frac{1}{4}$

4. Demetri needs to make 7 cups of coffee for his family's breakfast, but his coffee pot only makes $3\frac{1}{2}$ cups at a time. How many pots of coffee must he make to serve everyone?

   D. $\frac{1}{4} \div 2$

5. Blake and Jerome will split $\frac{1}{4}$ of a cherry pie. How much of the cherry pie will each get?

   E. $\frac{1}{2} \div 4$

6. Ella has $\frac{1}{2}$ teaspoon of salt left. If the salt must last 4 days, how much salt can she use each day?

   F. $\frac{1}{2} \div 4$

Helping at Home

Ask your child to think about what it means to divide a number by a fraction and think of a real-life example. For instance, dividing a one-hour chore into $\frac{1}{4}$ -hour segments yields four segments.

Word Problems with Fractions

Solve each problem. Write the answer in simplified form.

1. Of the 40 students who auditioned for the school play, $\frac{3}{4}$ of them were called back for a second audition. Of those called back, only $\frac{1}{3}$ received a part in the play. What fraction of those students who auditioned actually received a part in the play?

2. The main song in the play is a duet that is $2\frac{1}{2}$ minutes long. If the 2 singers get equal singing time, how many minutes does each sing?

3. The curtain on the stage is $15\frac{1}{2}$ feet tall, which is $\frac{1}{4}$ foot too short to hide all of the props. How tall does the curtain need to be to hide all of the props?

4. The entire play is $1\frac{3}{4}$ hours long, which is evenly divided among 3 acts. How long is each act?

5. The audience was composed of parents and students. There were 84 people enjoying the show. If $\frac{1}{3}$ of the audience was parents, how many students attended the play?

Helping at Home

Help your child find a food package that provides nutrition facts including serving size, grams of protein, grams of sodium, etc. Can your child write and solve three word problems based on the information that include fractions?

Converting Measurements

The chart shows the relationship between units of length in the customary measurement system.

Divide to change a smaller unit to a larger unit.

51 feet = ___ yards

Think: 3 ft. = 1 yd.
$51 \div 3 = 17$
51 ft. = 17 yd.

Units of Length
12 inches (in.) = 1 foot (ft.)
3 feet   = 1 yard (yd.)
36 inches   = 1 yard
5,280 feet   = 1 mile (mi.)
1,760 yards   = 1 mile

Multiply to change a larger unit to a smaller unit.

6 yards = ___ inches

Think: 1 yd. = 36 in.
$6 \times 36 = 216$
6 yd. = 216 in.

Circle the greater length.

1. 10 in. or 1 ft.

2. 3 ft. or 38 in.

3. 1 ft. 7 in. or 17 in.

4. 4 ft. 4 in. or 56 in.

5. 1 ft. 9 in. or 2 ft.

6. 7 ft. or 2 yd.

7. 6 yd. or 17 ft.

8. 26 in. or 2 ft.

9. 5 ft. or $1\frac{1}{2}$ yd.

10. 110 in. or 3 yd.

11. 5,000 ft. or 1 mi.

12. 11,000 ft. or 2 mi.

13. 5,000 yd. or 3 mi.

14. 7,020 ft. or 4 mi.

15. 3,200 yd. or 2 mi.

Write the equivalent measure.

16. 6 ft. = _____ in.

17. 72 in. = _____ yd.

18. 2 mi. = _____ yd.

19. 24 in. = _____ ft.

20. 18 ft. = _____ yd.

21. $1\frac{1}{2}$ ft. = _____ in.

22. 12 in. = _____ yd.

23. 2 mi. = _____ ft.

24 1 ft. 3 in. = _____ in.

25. 1 yd. 11 in. = _____ in.

26. 4 yd. = _____ ft.

27. $\frac{2}{3}$ yd. = _____ ft.

28. 60 in. = _____ ft.

29. 5,280 yd. = _____ mi.

30. 10 yd. = _____ in.

Helping at Home

Ask your child to use an online map to find the exact distance in miles between your home and his or her school. Can your child convert that distance into yards, feet, and inches? Can he or she convert the distance into meters and kilometers?

Converting Measurements

The amount of liquid a container can hold can be measured by using units such as the cup and the quart.

Many of the bottled liquids you buy in the store are measured in fluid ounces (fl. oz.). There are 8 fluid ounces in a cup, 16 fluid ounces in a pint, 32 fluid ounces in a quart, and 128 fluid ounces in a gallon.

Units of Capacity	
8 fluid ounces (fl. oz.)	= 1 cup
2 cups	= 1 pint (pt.)
16 fluid ounces	= 1 pint
2 pints	= 1 quart (qt.)
4 quarts	= 1 gallon (gal.)

Examples:

32 fl. oz. = _?_ cups
Think: 1 cup = 8 fl. oz. To change from a smaller unit to a larger unit, divide.
32 ÷ 8 = 4   32 fl. oz. = 4 cups

5 qt. = _?_ pt.
Think: 1 qt. = 2 pt. To change from a larger unit to a smaller unit, multiply.
5 × 2 = 10
5 qt. = 10 pt.

Choose the most reasonable unit of measure for each. Write *fl. oz., cup, pt., qt.,* or *gal.*

1. a canned soft drink _____   a pitcher of juice _____   a sip of water _____

2. the water in a bathtub _____   the amount of sugar in a cake recipe _____

Write the equivalent measure.

3. 1 qt. = _____ pt.

4. 32 fl. oz. = _____ cups

5. 2 cups = _____ pt.

6. 16 fl. oz. = _____ pt.

7. 3 gal. = _____ qt.

8. 1 pt. = _____ fl. oz.

9. $\frac{1}{2}$ gal. = _____ cups

10. $\frac{1}{2}$ gal. = _____ pt.

11. $\frac{1}{2}$ gal. = _____ qt.

12. 3 qt. = _____ pt.

13. 4 pt. = _____ gal.

14. 1 gal. = _____ fl. oz.

Compare using <, >, or =.

15. 10 fl. oz. ◯ 1 cup

16. 5 qt. ◯ 2 gal.

17. 2 cups ◯ 46 fl. oz.

18. 64 fl. oz. ◯ 2 qt.

19. 3 gal. ◯ 22 pt.

20. 12 pt. ◯ 3 gal.

Have your child experiment with water, measuring cups, and pitchers in the kitchen to confirm the information in the units of capacity conversion chart at the top of this page. Can he or she use a measuring spoon to find out how many tablespoons are in a cup?

Converting Measurements

The basic unit of weight in the customary measurement system is the pound.
- Four sticks of butter weigh 1 **pound**.
- A large truck weighs about 2 **tons**.

Example: 64 oz. = __?__ lb.
Think: 1 lb. = 16 oz.
64 ÷ 16 = 4
64 oz. = 4 lb.

Units of Weight
16 ounces (oz.) = 1 pound (lb.)
2,000 pounds = 1 ton

Write the equivalent weight.

1. 96 oz. = _____ lb.

2. 3 lb. = _____ oz.

3. 7 tons = _____ lb.

4. 1 ton = _____ oz.

5. 160 oz. = _____ lb.

6. 10,000 lb. = _____ tons

7. 16 lb. 5 oz. = _____ oz.

8. 9 lb. 3 oz. = _____ oz.

9. $2\frac{1}{2}$ tons = _____ lb.

Compare using <, >, or =.

10. 96 oz. ◯ 20 lb.

11. 80 oz. ◯ 6 lb.

12. 3 lb. ◯ 50 oz.

13. $1\frac{1}{2}$ tons ◯ 3,000 lb.

14. 320 oz. ◯ 10 lb.

15. 61 oz. ◯ 4 lb.

16. 82 oz. ◯ 5 lb.

17. 6 tons ◯ 10,000 lb.

18. 100 oz. ◯ 7 lb.

19. $\frac{1}{2}$ ton ◯ 1,000 lb.

20. 32,000 oz. ◯ 1 ton

21. 1,600 oz. ◯ 100 lb.

Solve each problem.

22. Shannon uses 30 inches of ribbon to make one bow. How many feet of ribbon are needed to make 10 bows?

23. At the end of a bike ride, everyone drank a 16-fluid-ounce bottle of sports drink. If 12 kids and 2 adults were on the bike ride, how many quarts of sports drink did the riders drink?

Line Plots

Place the liquid measurements in the beakers on the line plot. Use the line plot to answer the questions.

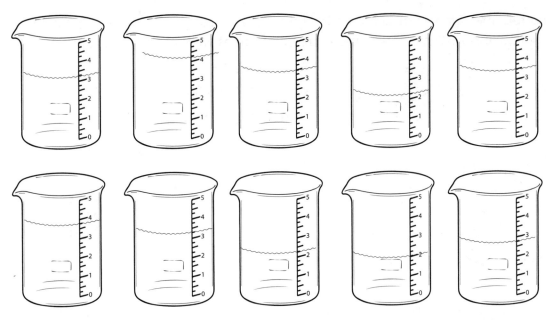

1.

2. How many beakers hold at least $2\frac{1}{2}$ ounces? What fraction of the set is that?	3. How much liquid does the set contain in all?
4. This set of beakers is a sample of a larger set. If the original set was 5 times larger, how much liquid did the original set contain?	5. If the liquid in this set was redistributed equally, how much liquid would each beaker contain?

Helping at Home

Ask your child to research local precipitation amounts for the past month and create a line plot to show the data. For each day, your child should write an X above the measurement (in fractions of an inch) that shows the precipitation amount.

Measuring Volume

Find the volume of each figure.

> **Volume** tells the number of cubic units within a solid figure. Each cube represents one cubic unit. To find volume, count the number of cubes within the figure.
>
>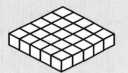
>
> There are 25 total cubes, so the volume is 25 cubic units.
>
> Volume (V) = 25 cubic units

Find the volume of each figure.

1.

V = _____ cubic units

2.

V = _____ cubic units

3.

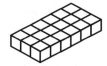

V = _____ cubic units

4.

V = _____ cubic units

5.

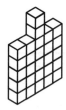

V = _____ cubic units

6.

V = _____ cubic units

Helping at Home

Provide a die and encourage your child to think of it as a "unit cube." Remember the properties of a cube. It has six square faces. Each side of each face of a unit cube measures 1 (for example: one inch or one centimeter).

Measuring Volume

Find the volume of each figure.

1.

V = _____ cubic units

2.

V = _____ cubic units

3.

V = _____ cubic units

4.

V = _____ cubic units

5.

V = _____ cubic units

6.

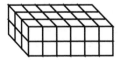

V = _____ cubic units

Helping at Home

For item #5 on this page, ask your child, "How many cubes wide is the figure? How many cubes long is the figure? How many cubes high is the figure?" Ask your child to multiply the three measurements. Is the result the same as the sum of the cubes?

Measuring Volume

Volume tells the number of cubic units within a solid figure. To find the volume of a rectangular prism, multiply the length by the width by the height ($V = l \times w \times h$).

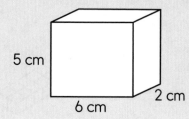

Volume (V) = $l \times w \times h$
V = 6 cm × 2 cm × 5 cm
V = 60 cm³

Find the volume of each figure. Label your answer.

1.
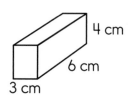

V = _____

2.
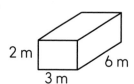

V = _____

3.
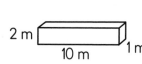

V = _____

4.
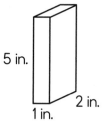

V = _____

5.
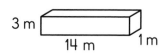

V = _____

6.
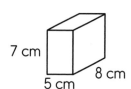

V = _____

7.
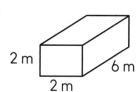

V = _____

8.
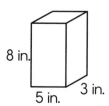

V = _____

Use the given dimensions to find the volume of each rectangular prism. Label your answer.

9. l = 2 cm
    w = 4 cm
    h = 3 cm

V = _____

10. l = 5 m
     w = 3 m
     h = 4 m

V = _____

11. l = 10 in.
     w = 3 in.
     h = 5 in.

V = _____

12. l = 3.5 ft.
     w = 1 ft.
     h = 2 ft.

V = _____

Ask your child to imagine designing a swimming pool for your yard or neighborhood. What could the dimensions of the pool be to fit the available space? What volume of water would the pool hold?

Measuring Volume

Volume = $l \times w \times h$

5 × 9 × n = 90

45 × n = 90

What, when multiplied by 45, equals 90?

n = 2

Complete the table with the missing measurements.

	Length	Width	Height	Volume
1.	4 inches	12 inches		48 cubic inches
2.	6 feet		3 feet	36 cubic feet
3.		9 centimeters	2 centimeters	54 cubic centimeters
4.	2 meters	2 meters	2 meters	
5.	4 inches		3 inches	84 cubic inches
6.	3 yards	6 yards		36 cubic yards
7.	9 inches	7 inches	7 inches	
8.		13 centimeters	4 centimeters	416 cubic centimeters
9.	3 feet		8 feet	192 cubic feet
10.	6 millimeters	5 millimeters	9 millimeters	

Helping at Home

Ask your child to measure the dimensions of a shoe box, cereal box, or other box found around your home. What is the volume of the box? Was it calculated in cubic inches, cubic feet, cubic centimeters, or some other unit?

Measuring Volume

For each problem, sketch a picture of the figure. Then, find the volume.

1. An aquarium is shaped like a rectangular prism and is 20 inches wide, 15 inches tall, and 15 inches long. How many cubic inches of water can the aquarium hold?

2. A moving box is 1 meter wide, $\frac{1}{2}$ meter long, and $\frac{3}{4}$ meter tall. How many cubic meters can the box hold?

3. A rectangular bathtub has dimensions of 2 feet deep by 2 feet wide by 5 feet long. If you only fill the bathtub to a depth of 18 inches, how many cubic inches of water is in the tub?

© Carson-Dellosa • CD-704505

Helping at Home

Help your child draw figures that have length, width, and height. Start with a box shape. You may wish to use an online tutorial for help with drawing three-dimensional figures. How does drawing help your child understand the concept of volume?

Measuring Volume

You can find the volume of more complex figures using addition.

First, split the shape into two rectangular prisms.

Then, find the volume of each prism.

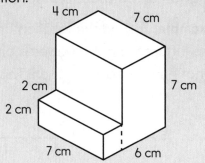

　　　2 cm × 2 cm × 7 cm = 28 cubic cm

　　　4 cm × 7 cm × 7 cm = 196 cubic cm

Finally, add the two volumes together.

　　　28 cubic cm + 196 cubic cm = 224 cubic cm

Find the volume of each figure.

1. 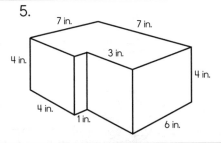	**2.** 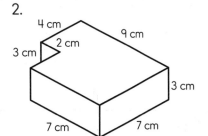
3. 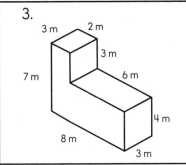	**4.** 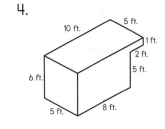
5.	**6.** 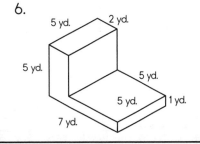

Helping at Home

Encourage your child to build a complex shape using books, boxes, or other box-shaped items. Can he or she take measurements in inches, calculate the volume of each box shape, and add to find the total volume?

Using a Grid

A **grid** can be used to show an object's location. It has numbered or lettered lines.

Example: To find the location of the , move along the bottom horizontal line and find the lettered line the flower is on. Then, move up the line vertically and trace across to see what numbered line it is on. This flower is located at (F, 3).

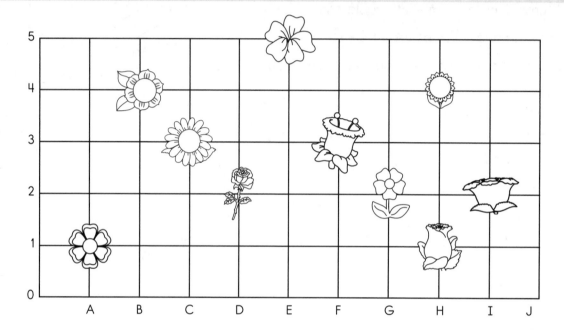

Use the grid above to write the location of each plant.

1. = (___ , ___)   2. 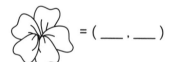 = (___ , ___)   3. 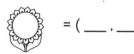 = (___ , ___)

4. = (___ , ___)   5. 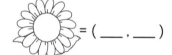 = (___ , ___)   6. = (___ , ___)

7. = (___ , ___)   8. = (___ , ___)   9. = (___ , ___)

Helping at Home
Use self-sticking notes or masking tape to label the lines on one side of a checkerboard A–H and the lines on the other side 1–8. Place a toy or other small item at the intersection of two squares. Can your child provide its coordinates?

Ordered Pairs

An **ordered pair** can be used to locate a point on a grid or coordinate graph. An ordered pair looks like this: (2,3). The first number tells how many units the point is located to the right of zero. The second number tells how many units the point is located up from zero.

Example: Find (2,3). Move right 2, and up 3.

Write the letter for each ordered pair.

1. (4,6) _____
2. (7,7) _____
3. (5,1) _____
4. (1,1) _____

5. (1,1) _____
6. (1,4) _____
7. (6,2) _____
8. (4,3) _____

9. (0,5) _____
10. (8,3) _____
11. (2,7) _____
12. (6,5) _____

13. (3,2) _____
14. (1,4) _____
15. (5,1) _____
16. (5,1) _____

17. (1,1) _____
18. (1,4) _____
19. (4,3) _____
20. (2,7) _____

21. (2,4) _____
22. (8,1) _____
23. (5,1) _____
24. (7,4) _____

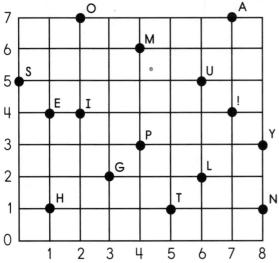

Write the letters above.
What is the secret message?

_____

_____

Helping at Home — Have your child use graph paper to create a large grid. Pin it to a bulletin board. Then, name ordered pairs such as (2, 6), (3, 7), (5, 1), and (8, 6). Challenge your child to insert a thumbtack at each point you name.

Ordered Pairs

An **ordered pair** can be used to locate a point on a grid or coordinate graph. An ordered pair looks like this: (2,4). The first number tells how many units the point is located to the right of zero. The second number tells how many units the point is located up from zero.

Example: Find (2,4). Move right 2, and up 4.

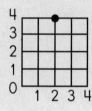

Write the letter for each ordered pair to find the message.

___ ___ ___ ___   ___ ___   ___ ___ ___   ___ ___   ___ ___ ___
(2,1) (4,5) (1,3) (8,3) (1,0) (4,1) (5,4) (7,1) (1,5) (5,4) (4,3) (1,3) (8,3) (1,5)

___ ___ ___ ___ ___ ___ ___ ___ ___ ___   ___ ___ ___
(1,0) (7,1) (7,4) (5,1) (1,5) (6,6) (1,0) (1,5) (7,1) (1,3) (4,1) (4,3) (5,4) (5,1)

___ ___ ___ ___ ___ ___
(2,1) (4,5) (6,3) (1,0) (7,1) (7,4)

___ ___ ___ ___   ___ ___ ___ ___
(1,2) (1,0) (4,3) (1,5) (4,3) (3,3) (7,1) (6,2)

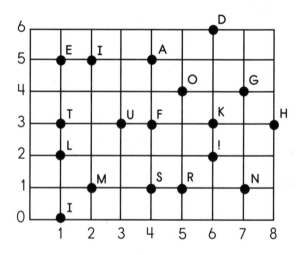

© Carson-Dellosa • CD-704505

Encourage your child to research and learn about imaginary latitude and longitude lines that cover the globe. How are they like a grid or coordinate graph? What are the coordinates of the place where you live?

Helping at Home

Polygons

A **polygon** is a closed plane figure formed by three or more line segments with two sides meeting at each vertex.

 triangle    **quadrilateral**   **square**   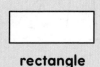 **rectangle**   **rhombus**

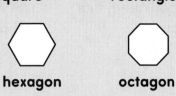 **parallelogram**   **pentagon**   **hexagon**   **octagon**   **trapezoid**

Identify each figure. Then, circle all of the quadrilaterals.

1.
_____

2.
_____

3.
_____

4.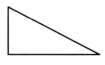
_____

5.
_____

6.
_____

7.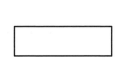
_____

8.
_____

9.
_____

10.
_____

11.
_____

12.
_____

Helping at Home

Can your child build each shape shown on this page from toothpicks or segments of drinking straws? How many sides does each shape have? How many vertexes does each shape have?

Attributes of Polygons

A **quadrilateral** has 4 sides.

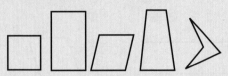

A **trapezoid** is a quadrilateral that has exactly 1 pair of parallel sides.

A **parallelogram** is a quadrilateral that has 2 pairs of parallel sides.

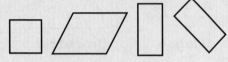

A **rectangle** is a parallelogram that has 4 right angles.

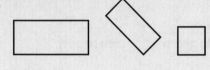

A **square** is a rectangle that has four equal sides.

Classify the following quadrilaterals. Some shapes may have more than one correct classification.

(A) quadrilateral   (B) trapezoid   (C) parallelogram   (D) rectangle   (E) square

1.    _____

2. 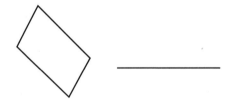   _____

3. 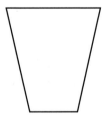   _____

4.   _____

5. 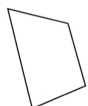   _____

6.   _____

Helping at Home

Give clues to one of the shapes shown on this page. Make sure your clues are very specific. For example, say, "It is a quadrilateral. It has two pairs of parallel sides. All sides are the same length." (Answer: square.) Have your child give you clues, too.

Quadrilaterals

Name the quadrilateral(s) described.

1. I have 4 sides and 4 right angles.

2. I have 4 sides, and opposite sides are parallel.

3. I have 4 sides and only 1 pair of parallel sides.

4. I have 4 congruent sides, and opposite sides are parallel.

5. I have 4 sides, 2 obtuse angles, and 2 acute angles.

6. I have 4 congruent sides, and opposite angles are equal.

Challenge your child to use a ruler to draw each quadrilateral described on this page. Ask him or her to label each drawing and display it somewhere in your home.

Answer Key

Page 11

1. Jess; 2. the pronoun I and the conversations; 3. Jess and Jim are siblings and are adventurous. Jess is younger and more cautious. Jim is older and brave. 4. Answers will vary, but possible answers include that the dialogue would be different, and the reader would know more of Jim's thoughts. 5. fast-moving water

Page 13

1. Jess becomes brave to help Jim. 2. Answers will vary. 3. Answers will vary. 4. Answers will vary, but possible answers include knowing more about Jim's thoughts or the pain Jim was in. 5. Answers will vary, but possible answers include being able to know more about what each of the characters were thinking.

Page 15

1. C; 2. Answers will vary, but possible answers include that the word shadow is used at the end of the third line of each stanza. Eldorado is used as the last word in each stanza. The rhyme scheme is aabccb. 3. Answers will vary, but possible answers include: for the rhythm and rhyme; to make it easier to read and understand. 4. He dies; "as his strength failed him at length"; 5. Answers will vary, but possible answers include that Poe might have been suggesting that people should pursue their dreams no matter how long it takes them, or that people should appreciate what they have and not waste their lives seeking unattainable treasures.

Page 17

1. Answers will vary, but possible answers include that a brave boy places his finger in a hole in a dike to keep the water from bursting through the dike and flooding the town. 2. A dike is a wall that holds back water. 3. Answers will vary. 4. B; 5. the voice of the ocean murmuring

Page 19

1. Answers will vary, but possible answers may include that Finlay and Murchadh are both kind. Finlay is young and Murchadh is old. 2. Finlay moves from one relative's home to another. Murchadh has lived in his home for a long time. 3. B; "Long ago" indicates it is not present day. The setting indicates it is not thousands or millions of years ago. 4. Answers will vary, but possible answers include being found by a kind shepherd.

Page 21

1. Answers will vary, but possible answers include that an orphan finds good fortune after being taken in by a kind shepherd and sleeping in a yew tree. 2. A; 3.

Folktale Characteristics	"The Hero of Harlem"	"The Yew Tree"
Ordinary Characters	a young boy	an orphan; a shepherd
Storyteller's Beginning	long ago	long ago
A Problem to Solve	hole in a dike	an unloved orphan
A Happy Ending	A boy saves the town.	An orphan finds gold and a home with a kind shepherd.
A Positive Theme	No one is too young to help.	Good things happen to good people.

Page 22

1. row of trees and soldiers standing at attention; Answers will vary. 2. cars and ants crawling along; Answers will vary. 3. clowns and sardines packed; Answers will vary. 4. shadows and ghosts dancing; Answers will vary; 5. sound of waves lapping and a dog getting a drink; Answers will vary; 6. baseball flew and rocket; Answers will vary.

Page 23

1. Laws are rules that help people live together. 2. Traffic laws keep people safe on the roads. Police officers enforce laws. Laws protect people's freedoms. 3. to protect the rights of all citizens

Answer Key

Page 25

1. nonfiction; real-life story; 2. She was awarded the Nobel Prize. She and her husband became known worldwide for their work studying radioactivity. 3. B; 4. Answers will vary, but possible events on the time line include: born on November 7, 1867; went to college in 1891; graduated in 1893; earned a second degree in 1894; married in 1895; died on July 4, 1934.

Page 27

1. He discovered a way to control silkworm disease. He developed vaccines. He developed the process of pasteurization. 2. a medical doctor; 3. People who earn advanced degrees are called doctors. 4. Answers will vary, but possible answers include yes, because they lived in France during the same time. 5. Answers will vary, but possible events on the time line include: Pasteur: born in 1822; opened a research center in 1888; died in 1895. Sklodowska: born in 1867; died in 1934.

Page 29

1. Answers will vary, but possible events on the time line include: saw first airplane in 1907; saw a stunt-flying exhibition in 1917; took flying lessons in 1921; 2. Answers will vary. 3. Answers will vary.

Page 31

1. He was an explorer of the western frontier and a fur trapper. (Child should include evidence from text to support the answers.) 2. Answers will vary, but possible answers include that they were both legendary, brave, and adventurous. 3. Answers will vary, but possible answers include that both passages are organized under subheadings. 4. The headings in "A Pioneer of Flight" are organized chronologically; in "John Colter: Western Explorer," the headings are organized by topic.

Page 33

Answers will vary.

Page 35

1. Chinese immigrants were treated unfairly in the late 1800s and early 1900s. 2. C; 3. G; 4. E; 5. F; 6. H; 7. D; 8. A; 9. B

Page 37

1. Chinese immigration in the early 1900s; 2. to inform the reader about the unfair treatment of Chinese immigrants; 3. Answers will vary, but possible answers may include that both passages tell that Angel Island was an immigration station for Chinese immigrants beginning in 1910. 4. Answers will vary, but possible answers may include "Immigration at Angel Island" provides more information about the discrimination of the Chinese immigrants through the Chinese Exclusion Act. 5. Answers will vary, but possible answers may include "Poems from Angel Island" includes information about how the Chinese immigrants felt about being detained on Angel Island.

Page 38

Answers will vary.

Page 39

Answers will vary.

Page 40

Answers will vary.

Page 41

Answers will vary.

Page 42

Answers will vary.

Page 43

Answers will vary.

Page 44

Answers will vary, but possible answers are included below. Did you know that you can plant a sunflower seed inside a cup? It is simple and fun! First, gather the following materials: a clear, plastic cup; a wet paper towel; and a sunflower seed. Next, place the paper towel inside the cup. At this point, make sure that the paper

Answer Key

towel covers the entire inside of the cup. Place the seed on the paper towel and fold the paper towel over the seed. Then, place the cup near a window with a lot of sunlight shining through. If your sunflower does not get enough sunlight, it will not be able to grow. It will take three weeks for your seed to sprout. In the meantime, you can record any changes that you observe. Finally, you will be able to see your sunflower flourish.

Page 45
Answers will vary.

Page 46
1. Answers will vary, but possible descriptions may include cold, musty, drafty, or chilly. 2. Answers will vary, but possible descriptions may include bright, tall, quiet, or worn down. 3. Answers will vary, but possible descriptions may include colorful, aromatic, fresh, or beautiful. 4. Answers will vary, but possible descriptions may include tight, squishy, smelly, or hot.

Page 47
Answers will vary.

Page 48
Setting: Dike in Harlem, Holland; Characters: Hans, his younger brother, the townspeople; Problem:

There was a hole in the dike. Event 1: Hans put his finger in the hole. Event 2: Hans's brother ran to get help. Event 3: The townspeople came. Solution: The dike was fixed and Hans was a hero.

Page 49
1. Sarah wanted to go swimming, but it rained. 2. The car broke down, so I took a taxi. 3. The man was tired, so he sat on a bench. 4. It started raining, so I opened my umbrella. 5. I watered the plant, but it wilted. 6. The baby cried because she was hungry. 7. Jeremy bought some milk although he still had some left. 8. The boy started a new painting while his first painting was drying.

Page 50
1. Well,; 2. Wow,; 3. Yes,; 4. Phew,; 5. No,; 6. Wow,; 7. Yes,; 8. Wait,; 9. Hey,; 10. Great,

Page 51
1. in; 2. around; 3. in; 4. near; 5. on; 6. at; 7. in; 8. to; 9. Wow, there is a lot to learn about the solar system. 10. Our group made models of Mars, Earth, and Venus. 11. Oh no, our models of Earth and Venus fell apart, but the model of Mars is fine. 12. Jeremy, would you like to travel to Mars or Venus some day? 13. The planets, moons, and stars are part of the solar system. 14. Don't you think this has been an

interesting unit, Robert?

Page 52
1. have/has walked, had walked, will have walked; 2. have/has run, had run, will have run; 3. have/has jumped, had jumped, will have jumped; 4. have/has skipped, had skipped, will have skipped; 5. have/has hopped, had hopped, will have hopped; 6. have/has joined, had joined, will have joined; 7. will have learned; 8. have learned; 9. had learned

Page 53
1. Scientists have learned that rhinoceroses have lived on Earth for about 40 million years. 2. Fossils show that there were more than 30 species of rhinos. 3. A rhinoceros ranks as one of the largest land creatures. 4. Most wild rhinos live in Africa, southeastern Asia, and Sumatra. 5. Indian rhinos have skin that looks like a suit of armor. 6. They inhabit marshy jungles among reeds and tall grasses. 7. Illegal hunters, called poachers, have hunted rhinos for their valuable horns for many years. 8. Some people grind up rhino horns to treat sicknesses.

Page 54
1. Neither/nor; 2. Both/and; 3. either/or; 4. Both/and; 5. neither/nor; 6. both/and; 7. Either/or; 8. Neither/nor; 9.

© Carson-Dellosa • CD-704505

Answer Key

Both/and; 10. either/or

Page 55

1. Hayden ordered lasagna, salad, and milk for dinner. 2. Hayden likes zucchini, but he does not like beans, peas, or spinach. 3. Hayden couldn't decide whether to have the chocolate, strawberry, or vanilla yogurt for dessert. 4. Peaches, pears, and grapes are my favorite fruits. 5. Which do you like most, peaches, pears, or grapes? 6. My mother made a fruit salad with apples, bananas, strawberries, and grapes. 7. Nicole, Marisa, and I enjoyed eating the fruit salad.

Page 56

1. Because my dad was a Boy Scout, our family lives by the motto, "Be prepared." 2. Until my sister is a little older, my parents will not take us to the amusement park. 3. Before we leave to go anywhere, we lock the door to our house. 4. After hearing about the fire at our neighbor's house, my family made an emergency plan. 5. Because my cousin is allergic to peanuts, we cannot have peanuts in our home. 6. Yes, my family must arrive at the airport at least two hours before our flight leaves. 7. Although I think my family is a bit too cautious, I appreciate the care they have for me. 8. Is your family as cautious as

my family, Claire? 9. Jose, you will have to leave by seven o'clock.

Page 57

1. "The Ugly Duckling"; 2. "The Lion's Share"; 3. "The Fir Tree"; 4. "Shooting Stars"; 5. "Always Wondering"; 6. "Floradora Doe"; 7. "Down in the Valley"; 8. "Go Tell Aunt Rhody"; 9. "Monster Mash"; 10. Our class read the story "The Golden Touch." 11. We sang the "Star Spangled Banner" at the baseball game. 12. I memorized the entire poem "Paul Revere's Ride."

Page 58

Kelly, Aaron, Brandon, and I are best <u>friends</u>. We are in the same class at school. We have so much fun when we are together. We wanted to go to the movies, so we asked our parents. After our parents agreed to take us, we decided on a movie and made plans to meet at the theater Saturday afternoon. Kelly arrived first, and Aaron and Brandon arrived <u>immediately</u> after. As usual, I was late. By the time I got <u>there</u>, <u>everyone</u> was in line to buy snacks. They knew better than to wait for me. Brandon ordered nachos, popcorn, and a large lemonade. I could not <u>believe</u> that he planned to eat so much. "I'm a growing boy," Brandon always said. The rest of us decided to share a large <u>popcorn</u>.

Then it was time to find our seats. The theater was so dark we couldn't see <u>anything</u>. We stumbled in and sat in the first row. Luckily, the theater was empty <u>because</u> we spent the entire time whispering and <u>giggling</u>. I could not even tell you what the movie was about. After it ended, our parents picked us up. We said <u>good-bye</u> and headed home. If our parents agree, we will get together <u>again</u> next weekend and go bowling. <u>It's</u> fun to have best friends.

Page 59

1. fabulous; 2. handsomely; 3. eagerly; 4. talented; 5. huge; 6. absolutely; 7. magnificently; 8. brilliantly; 9. enthusiastically; 10. splendid; 11. delicate; 12. joyously; 13. difficult; 14. outstanding; 15. beautifully; 16. remarkably; 17. world-famous; 18. successfully

Page 60

1. B; 2. D; 3. A; 4. E; 5. C; 6–8. Answers will vary.

Page 61

1. E, N; 2. B, H; 3. L, R; 4. A, P; 5. F, T; 6. C, O; 7. K, M; 8. D, I; 9. G, Q; 10. J, S

Page 62

1. F; 2. C; 3. A; 4. E; 5. D; 6. B; 7. H; 8. J; 9. K; 10. G; 11. L; 12. I

Answer Key

Page 63

1. young; 2. sigh; 3. view;
4. rip; 5. laugh; 6. hideous;
7. unsociable; 8. loose; 9.
gliding; 10. enthusiastic;
11. gathers; 12. tardy; 13.
ordinary; 14. party; 15. slice;
16. built

Page 68

1. 4; 2. 6; 3. 24; 4. 90; 5. 100;
6. 200

Page 69

1. 10; 2. 45; 3. 36; 4. 15; 5. 96;
6. 16; 7. 5; 8. 19

Page 70

1. $(5 + 6) \times 3$; 2. $(15 - 7) \times 4$;
3. $2 \times [20 - (6 + 10)]$; 4. $(5 + 6) \times (3 + 4)$; 5. $(4 + 6) \times 7$; 6.
$(5 + 9) \div 2$

Page 71

1. H; 2. A; 3. G; 4. B; 5. F; 6. C;
7. E; 8. D

Page 72

1. albums increase by 1,
records increase by 2
million; 2. 1, 3, 5, 7, 9; 3. (2,3),
(3,5), (4,7), (5,9); 4. Check
child's graph. 5. 9

Page 73

1. laps increase by 2, breaths
increase by 1; 2. 2, 3, 4, 5,
6; 3. (2,2), (4,3), (6,4), (8,5),
(10,6); 4. Check child's
graph. 5. 6

Page 74

1. 8.5; 2. 50; 3. 23.5; 4. 50;
5. 15.3; 6. 512.5; 7. 150.3; 8.
Answers will vary.

Page 75

1. 0.6, 6, 60, 6; 2. 43, 430,
4,300, 43; 3. 653, 10.9, 213,
0.07; 4. 46, 460, 46, 4.6; 5.
3,900, 0.045, 3, 12,600; 6.
123.4, 110, 1,100, 11,000

Page 76

1. two places right; 2. five
places right; 3. three places
left; 4. one place left; 5. two
places left; 6. two places
right; 7. four places right; 8.
four places left

Page 77

1. $\frac{3}{10}$; 2. one and twelve
hundredths, $1\frac{12}{100}$; 3. 0.221,
$\frac{221}{1000}$

Page 78

1. <; 2. <; 3. <; 4. >; 5. >; 6. >; 7.
>; 8. >; 9. <; 10. <; 11. <; 12. =; 13.
<; 14. >; 15. =; 16. <

Page 79

1. 0.6; 2. 1.0; 3. 1.6; 4. 3.1; 5.
6.35; 6. 3.15; 7. 0.01; 8. 2.59; 9.
3.0, 3.02; 10. 30.0, 29.96

Page 80

1. 290,322; 2. 372,723;
3. 572,286; 4. 856,304;
5. 260,766; 6. 82,369;
7. 332,762; 8. 136,125; 9.
236,572; 10. 171,720; 11. 39,449;
12. 157,320; 13. 380,328; 14.
315,864; 15. 750,339; 16.
1,101,790; 17. 1,210,808; 18.
480,075; 19. 385,985; 20.
547,328

Page 81

1. 18r29; 2. 22r19; 3. 260r9; 4.
31r23; 5. 222r8; 6. 252r3; 7.
42r3; 8. 122r61

Page 82

S 1,944; O 104r2; E 57,762; Y
4r1; K 1,484; A 61r4; D 28,288;
W 6r52; J 138,788; U 453r2;
F 5,844; L 10,080; T 98r42; N
61,318; C 237r11; R 209,746; I
106r29; H 236r13; just fine,
tanks; worse dish year;
classy

Page 83

1. $23.74; 2. $40.79; 3. $74.71;
4A. $46.05; B. 42.5 mph

Page 84

1. 1,596.8, 159.68, 15.968,
159.68, 1.5968; 2. 1,802.4,
180.24, 18.024, 180.24, 1.8024;
3. 1,251.0, 125.10, 12.510, 125.10,
1.2510; 4. 7.92, 25.56, 13.09,
8.76, 69.84; 5. 91.14, 138.82,
172.02, 21.142, 9.971

Page 85

1. $1.88 \times 1.2 = 2.256$; 2. $5.19 \times 0.32 = 1.6608$; 3. $8.76 \times 4.3 = 37.668$; 4. $25.6 \times 3.1 = 79.36$;
5. $4.32 \times 2.1 = 9.072$; 6. $14.9 \times 2.7 = 40.23$; 7. $1.51 \times 4.5 = 6.795$; 8. $3.12 \times 0.61 = 1.9032$

Page 86

1. 0.54; 2. 1.15; 3. 0.95; 4. 1.825;
5. 0.3125; 6. 0.0775; 7. 1.62;
8. 1.575; 9. 0.146; 10. 1.05; 11.
0.838; 12. 0.748; 13. 13.35; 14.
0.065; 15. 15.004

Answer Key

Page 87

1. 9; 2. 0.2; 3. 9.9; 4. 0.85; 5. 6.2; 6. 7; 7. 5; 8. 38; 9. 3; 10. 4.3; 11. 15; 12. 0.3125

Page 88

1. 200 trombones; 2. 0.055 watts; 3. about 28 pianos; 4A. 19.14 watts; B. 6.38 watts; 5. 11 pianos

Page 89

1. 6, $\frac{4}{6}$, $\frac{5}{6}$; 2. 4, $\frac{2}{4}$, $\frac{1}{4}$; 3. 10, $\frac{4}{10}$, $\frac{1}{10}$; 4. 12, $\frac{9}{12}$, $\frac{1}{12}$; 5. 14, $\frac{14}{14}$, $\frac{2}{14}$; 6. 9, $\frac{6}{9}$, $\frac{3}{9}$; 7. 10, $\frac{1}{10}$, $\frac{6}{10}$; 8. 6, $\frac{4}{6}$, $\frac{3}{6}$; 9. 20, $\frac{15}{20}$, $\frac{12}{20}$

Page 90

1. 5$\frac{13}{24}$; 2. 5$\frac{19}{20}$; 3. 7$\frac{1}{6}$; 4. 5$\frac{11}{12}$; 5. 7$\frac{1}{4}$; 6. 7$\frac{11}{15}$; 7. 6$\frac{1}{12}$; 8. 4$\frac{11}{24}$; 9. 7$\frac{1}{4}$; 10. 5$\frac{1}{10}$; 11. 9$\frac{7}{8}$; 12. 12$\frac{3}{22}$

Page 91

1. $\frac{5}{12}$; 2. $\frac{3}{10}$; 3. $\frac{1}{6}$; 4. $\frac{3}{14}$; 5. $\frac{5}{18}$; 6. $\frac{11}{21}$; 7. $\frac{18}{20}$; 8. $\frac{11}{35}$; 9. $\frac{17}{45}$; 10. $\frac{19}{40}$; 11. $\frac{29}{42}$; 12. $\frac{43}{66}$

Page 92

1. 4$\frac{1}{8}$; 2. 2$\frac{2}{3}$; 3. 5$\frac{2}{9}$; 4. 3$\frac{3}{5}$; 5. 7$\frac{1}{5}$; 6. 4$\frac{5}{9}$; 7. 11$\frac{8}{11}$; 8. 8$\frac{7}{9}$; 9. 6$\frac{2}{3}$; 10. 9$\frac{4}{5}$; 11. 11$\frac{3}{10}$; 12. 7$\frac{1}{6}$

Page 93

1. 1$\frac{5}{6}$; 2. $\frac{23}{24}$; 3. 1$\frac{3}{14}$; 4. 3$\frac{4}{15}$; 5. $\frac{5}{8}$; 6. $\frac{5}{9}$; 7. $\frac{5}{16}$; 8. 1$\frac{7}{10}$; 9. 1$\frac{17}{24}$; 10. 3$\frac{3}{8}$; 11. 3$\frac{1}{2}$; 12. $\frac{3}{4}$

Page 94

1. $\frac{5}{12}$; 2A. $\frac{11}{12}$; B. $\frac{1}{12}$; 3A. $\frac{3}{4}$; B. $\frac{1}{4}$; 4. 6$\frac{1}{3}$ minutes

Page 95

1. 3$\frac{11}{12}$ hours; 2. $\frac{7}{12}$ hours; 3. $\frac{2}{3}$ hours; 4. 2$\frac{5}{12}$ hours; 5. 1$\frac{1}{12}$ hours; 6. Tyrone

Page 96

1. 7$\frac{1}{2}$; 2. 1$\frac{3}{4}$; 3. 2$\frac{6}{7}$; 4. 8$\frac{3}{5}$; 5. 2$\frac{7}{8}$; 6. 4$\frac{5}{8}$; 7. 2$\frac{7}{12}$; 8. 2$\frac{2}{2}$; 9. $\frac{5}{18}$; 10. 2$\frac{3}{4}$; 11. 5$\frac{4}{9}$; 12. 6$\frac{5}{6}$; 13. 7$\frac{2}{3}$; 14. 11$\frac{3}{4}$; 15. 12

Page 97

1. $\frac{1}{4}$ pie; 2. $\frac{2}{3}$ cup; 3. 1$\frac{1}{2}$ cups; 4. $\frac{1}{2}$ foot; 5. 6$\frac{1}{4}$ pounds; 6. 1$\frac{1}{3}$ cups

Page 98

1. $\frac{2}{15}$; 2. $\frac{1}{12}$; 3. $\frac{1}{4}$; 4. $\frac{3}{8}$

Page 99

1. $\frac{3}{8}$; 2. $\frac{2}{15}$; 3. $\frac{2}{15}$; 4. $\frac{5}{12}$; 5. $\frac{3}{32}$; 6. $\frac{5}{24}$; 7. $\frac{5}{14}$; 8. $\frac{1}{12}$; 9. $\frac{2}{25}$; 10. $\frac{3}{10}$; 11. $\frac{9}{20}$; 12. $\frac{3}{32}$; 13. $\frac{6}{25}$; 14. $\frac{1}{4}$; 15. $\frac{4}{9}$; 16. $\frac{5}{16}$; 17. $\frac{5}{21}$; 18. $\frac{3}{14}$; 19. $\frac{5}{24}$; 20. $\frac{5}{18}$

Page 100

1. 10; 2. 3$\frac{1}{4}$; 3. 4$\frac{19}{20}$; 4. 2$\frac{3}{5}$; 5. 2$\frac{6}{25}$; 6. 8$\frac{3}{4}$; 7. 7$\frac{7}{2}$; 8. 14$\frac{7}{10}$; 9. 5$\frac{13}{24}$; 10. 2$\frac{1}{4}$; 11. 1$\frac{27}{28}$; 12. 5$\frac{1}{2}$; 13. 6$\frac{1}{10}$; 14. 9$\frac{1}{3}$

Page 101

1. 1$\frac{1}{6}$ cups; 2. $\frac{3}{8}$ teaspoons chili powder, 2$\frac{1}{4}$ tablespoons olive oil; 3. 2 ounces, 2; 4. 1$\frac{1}{3}$; 5. 1$\frac{7}{9}$ cups; 6. 2 cups; 7. 401°

Page 102

1. $\frac{4}{9}$; 2. $\frac{1}{2}$; 3. 5$\frac{3}{25}$

Page 103

1. 13$\frac{1}{2}$; 2. 35; 3. $\frac{1}{4}$; 4. $\frac{3}{5}$; 5. $\frac{3}{20}$; 6. $\frac{1}{8}$; 7. $\frac{9}{40}$; 8. $\frac{1}{18}$; 9. $\frac{3}{8}$; 10. $\frac{5}{12}$; 11. $\frac{4}{15}$; 12. $\frac{8}{25}$

Page 104

1. C, 8 pieces; 2. A, $\frac{1}{2}$ cup; 3. E, 8 glasses; 4. B, 2 pots; 5. D, $\frac{1}{8}$ pie; 6. F, $\frac{1}{8}$ teaspoon

Page 105

1. $\frac{1}{4}$; 2. 1$\frac{1}{4}$ minutes; 3. 15$\frac{3}{4}$ feet; 4. $\frac{7}{12}$ hour, or 35 minutes; 5. 56 students

Page 106

1. 1 ft. 2. 38 in. 3. 1 ft. 7 in. 4. 56 in. 5. 2 ft. 6. 7 ft. 7. 6 yd. 8. 26 in. 9. 5 ft. 10. 110 inches; 11. 1 mi. 12. 11,000 ft. 13. 3 mi. 14. 4 mi. 15. 2 mi. 16. 72; 17. 2; 18. 3,520; 19. 2; 20. 6; 21. 18; 22. $\frac{1}{3}$; 23. 10,560; 24. 15; 25. 47; 26. 12; 27. 2; 28. 5; 29. 3; 30. 360

Page 107

1. fluid ounces, quarts, fluid ounces; 2. gallons, cups; 3. 2; 4. 4; 5. 1; 6. 1; 7. 12; 8. 16; 9. 8;

Answer Key

10. 4; 11. 2; 12. 6; 13. $\frac{1}{2}$; 14. 128; 15. >; 16. <; 17. <; 18. =; 19. >; 20. <

Page 108

1. 6; 2. 48; 3. 14,000; 4. 32,000; 5. 10; 6. 5; 7. 261; 8. 147; 9. 5,000; 10. <; 11. <; 12. <; 13. =; 14. >; 15. <; 16. >; 17. >; 18. <; 19. =; 20. =; 21. =; 22. 25 feet; 23. 7 quarts

Page 109

1.

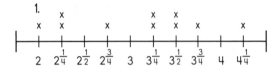

2. 7, $\frac{7}{10}$; 3. 30$\frac{3}{4}$ ounces; 4. 153$\frac{3}{4}$ ounces; 5. 3$\frac{3}{40}$ ounces

Page 110

1. 20; 2. 12; 3. 18; 4. 18; 5. 27; 6. 20

Page 111

1. 13; 2. 14; 3. 20; 4. 10; 5. 20; 6. 36

Page 112

1. 72 cubic centimeters; 2. 36 cubic meters; 3. 20 cubic meters; 4. 10 cubic inches; 5. 42 cubic meters; 6. 280 cubic centimeters; 7. 24 cubic meters; 8. 120 cubic inches; 9. 24 cubic centimeters; 10. 60 cubic meters; 11. 150 cubic inches; 12. 7 cubic feet

Page 113

1. 1 in. 2. 2 ft. 3. 3 cm; 4. 8 cubic meters; 5. 7 inches; 6. 2 yards; 7. 441 cubic inches; 8. 8 centimeters; 9. 8 feet; 10. 270 cubic millimeters

Page 114

1. 4,500 cubic inches; 2. $\frac{3}{8}$ cubic meter; 3. 25,920 cubic inches

Page 115

1. 38 cubic inches; 2. 171 cubic cm; 3. 114 cubic m; 4. 250 cubic feet; 5. 184 cubic inches; 6. 75 cubic yards

Page 116

1. (D,2); 2. (E,5); 3. (H,4); 4. (H,1); 5. (C,3); 6. (I,2); 7. (B,4); 8. (G,2); 9. (A,1)

Page 117

1. M; 2. A; 3. T; 4. H; 5. H; 6. E; 7. L; 8. P; 9. S; 10. Y; 11. O; 12. U; 13. G; 14. E; 15. T; 16. T; 17. H; 18. E; 19. P; 20. O; 21. I; 22. N; 23. T; 24. !; Math helps you get the point!

Page 118

Math is one of the ingredients for making life fun!

Page 119

1. rhombus; 2. octagon; 3. trapezoid; 4. triangle; 5. square; 6. pentagon; 7. rectangle; 8. parallelogram; 9. hexagon; 10. triangle; 11. quadrilateral; 12. parallelogram

Page 120

1. A, C, D; 2. A, C; 3. A, B; 4. A, C; 5. A, B; 6. A, C, D, E

Page 121

1. rectangle or square; 2. square, rectangle, parallelogram, or rhombus; 3. trapezoid; 4. square or rhombus; 5. parallelogram or rhombus; 6. square, rectangle, parallelogram, or rhombus